A Young Woman's Guide to Health and Well-Being

The
Yoga
Handbook

Dedicated to my beloved GURUDEV
His Holiness Sri Swami Satchidananda
You are my heart

A Young Woman's Guide to Health and Well-Being

The Yoga Handbook

Sumukhi Finney

ROSEN
PUBLISHING®

New York

This edition published in 2010 by:

The Rosen Publishing Group, Inc.
29 East 21st Street
New York, NY 10010

Library of Congress Cataloging-in-Publication Data

Finney, Sumukhi.
The yoga handbook / Sumukhi Finney.
      p. cm.—(A young woman's guide to health and well-being)
Includes bibliographical references and index.
ISBN-13: 978-1-4358-5359-1 (library binding)
1. Hatha yoga—Handbooks, manuals, etc. 2. Young women—Health and
hygiene—Handbooks, manuals, etc. I. Title.
 RA781.7.F57 2010
 613.7'046—dc22

                                                                2009010509

Manufactured in China

Contents

Introduction

Like a lot of people attending their first yoga class, I knew very little about the subject and didn't know what to expect. A friend had invited me along after I had been bending her ear one rainy afternoon, complaining about my lot in life. I always seemed to be tired, and didn't really feel happy; I felt something was missing, but I didn't know what. My friend had assured me that the yoga postures and relaxation would do me a world of good. I wanted to get fit and lose weight, as like many of us, I was not contented with how I looked and thought that if I had the "perfect" body all would be well. How was yoga going to help me, I wondered? How were gentle postures and relaxing going to shift those unwanted pounds and make me feel happy and contented?

I arrived at the class, positioned my mat so I would have a good view of what was going on, and made myself comfortable. The atmosphere in the room was calm and peaceful, and I instantly felt at ease. The other students were friendly and seemed to be eagerly awaiting their teacher as if a real treat were in store for them.

Edith, who was a wonderful yoga teacher with 20 years experience, walked in gracefully. With a loving, accepting smile, she took up her position at the front of the class and began to explain what yoga was all about.

Although I was finding out about yoga for the first time, it felt as if Edith was telling me something I already knew. The yogic view of the world and our place in it seemed to make complete sense. It was like finding and putting into place the last piece of a jigsaw puzzle. My first yoga class changed my life forever. After just one lesson, I felt physically comfortable—a new experience for me. I felt more accepting of myself. I felt stronger, yet more relaxed. I couldn't explain why but I felt happier and knew that I had to find out more about the practice of yoga.

I began to attend classes regularly and to study books on the subject, eager to learn and to experience more of the peace and contentment that yoga was bringing into my life. Through various yogic practices, including diet, breathing, meditation, and postures, as well as applying some basic moral and ethical principles, I gained a greater understanding and acceptance of myself and of the world around me. Before practicing yoga, I had tremendous difficulty in expressing my feelings and with communicating negative emotions. I avoided confrontation at any cost. Due to low self-esteem and a distorted view of myself physically, I had been plagued with bulimia for years, not even accepting that I had a problem. By applying yogic principles to my life, I began to communicate with honesty and courage. This helped to transform my relationships, resulting in greater self-expression and love. I began to experience inner peace, contentment, and acceptance, which gradually helped me to overcome the bulimia. I learned how to have a healthy balanced diet; I could finally eat what I wanted without guilt. I began to love my body, which began to change shape through my work with the postures. I was happy! Life still had and has its challenges and its ups and downs, but yoga has given me the tools to deal effectively with it. During 18 years of studying yoga, I have been fortunate to maintain this experience of health, happiness, peace, and contentment.

Yoga can help balance your mind and body, to give a sense of "wholeness" and great happiness.

After a couple of years, I wanted to find out and experience more about yoga and so I decided to train as a yoga teacher. I studied with the British Wheel of Yoga for two years, but although I completed the course, I did not complete the written work. Only now, 16 years later, have I become a recognized BWY teacher. Toward the end of my BWY training course, I went to a yoga conference in Zinal, Switzerland. I had begun to get a little disillusioned with yoga because I had got wrapped up in the theory. I wanted to experience yoga, not write about it. The European Yoga Conference was another changing point in my life because it was there that I met my Guru, His Holiness Sri Swami Satchidananda, known as Gurudev to his disciples, devotees, and students.

Sri Swami Satchidananda, known as Gurudev.

Gurudev is the founder and spiritual head of Integral Yoga® (see chapter 3). My heart melted, and I felt so peaceful in the presence of his unconditional love and peaceful nature. His sense of humor and the simple and practical way in which he was able to put across the ancient teachings of yoga convinced me that this was what I wanted to study and teach. I completed my first teacher training with Integral Yoga® in 1989 and have been studying, applying, and sharing the teachings of Sri Swami Satchidananda ever since.

Through this book, I would like to share some of the little I know in the hope that you are inspired to embark upon a journey that will bring greater health and happiness. Whether you are young, old, fat, thin, healthy, sick, black, white, Christian, Muslim . . . if you would like to benefit from a healthier and happier life, then this book is for you. It is suitable for newcomers as the posture section is based on a beginners' class, but there are also some challenging variations for the more experienced yogi. In addition to the physical side of yoga, this book also provides a good grounding in yogic philosophy and psychology. It will introduce you to the wider practices of yoga and thus enhance all areas of your life.

1

Yoga Schools and Styles

Before getting into what yoga is all about, we will take a brief look at some of the various yoga schools. At the moment, yoga is the latest craze—the "fashionable" thing to do. Yoga classes can be found in most sport and leisure centers, health clubs, adult education centers, and many community and church halls.

It is a good idea to go to a yoga class for many reasons. It gives you a set time for regular practice—something that not everyone finds easy to stick to at home. You can make sure you are doing the postures correctly. You can experience a greater sense of peace and calm as you are led through the postures without having to continually look at the description and pictures in a book. If you find that you are interested in your spiritual development, it's good to have a spiritual family, or *sangha*, a group of like-minded people who share your experiences and learn from each other.

Make sure your teacher is properly qualified. If the postures are taught incorrectly, you are likely to injure yourself.

Although you can practice your postures at home, a regular class helps you keep a regular routine, and it can be much more enjoyable sharing your efforts with a group of friends!

If you don't like your first class, try a different style of yoga—there are many to choose from and they do vary. But perhaps more important than style is the teacher–student relationship. Find a teacher who inspires you, a teacher with whom you feel confident and comfortable. Be willing and open to learn—some students are more interested in teaching the teacher, but you won't learn much that way!

The postures of yoga are Hatha yoga, although the way they are taught may differ according to the style of yoga.

The yoga postures you practice when you go to a class are those of Hatha yoga. However, there are many different approaches to teaching the postures. Some schools are very vigorous and give you more of a workout, while others concentrate on perfecting the form of the posture. Some styles focus on co-ordination of movement and breath; others focus on doing fewer postures but holding them for longer. There are schools that use sequences of postures and some that are very gentle. Some teach postures with a little relaxation, while other schools give a more balanced session, working on relaxation, breathing practices, and meditation. Some schools bring in a little philosophy and psychology, introducing the students to the wider practices of yoga. You need to decide what it is that you are looking to gain from your yoga class. Yoga is suitable for everyone, so keep looking until you find a teacher or school/style of yoga that suits you.

Your yoga teacher should provide inspiration and support.

Yoga Styles

Ananda Yoga

Developed by Swami Kriyananda, a disciple of Paramahansa Yogananda—founder and spiritual head of The Self-Realization Fellowship and author of the famous *Autobiography of a Yogi*. This is a more gentle style of yoga that focuses on inner experience and is concerned with awakening subtle energies, particularly within the chakras (see chapter 8). Ananda yoga uses asanas and pranayama to gain control over the subtle energies, bringing harmony to body, mind, and the emotions.

Ashtanga Yoga

Developed by K. Pattabhi Jois, this school focuses on a flow of postures, jumping from one pose to the next. Ashtanga yoga provides the practitioner with a thorough "workout" and is not for the faint-hearted or for the beginner. It helps to build stamina, flexibility, and strength.

Bikram Yoga

This school was developed by Bikram Choudhry, the founder of the Yoga College of India. The students work through a demanding series of 26 postures in a heated room. The series is designed to systematically work all muscles, tendons, joints, ligaments, internal organs, and glands and to encourage the release of toxins through sweating. The heated environment also allows the muscles to relax, avoiding strain, and helps with the healing of existing injuries. Breathing and concentration are an important part of a Bikram yoga class, as well as relaxing between each pose to assimilate the benefits and rejuvenate the body.

Desikachar Method

Carrying on his father's tradition (see Viniyoga, page 14), T.K.V. Desikachar teaches in the Viniyoga style, harmonizing sequences of postures with awareness of the breath. Classes usually include relaxation and meditation.

Kripalu Yoga

This gentler style of yoga coordinates breath and movement and is practiced in three stages. The beginner works on learning the postures, accepting and understanding the body's ability without competition. Progressing to stage two, the student holds the postures for longer and begins to develop greater concentration and inner awareness, understanding how the poses are working physically and psychologically. In the final stage, the student performs the postures as a moving meditation with the mind focused and the body and breath in harmony.

Integral Yoga®

Inspired by his Master, His Holiness Sri Swami Sivananda of Rishikesh, Himalayas, the founder of the Divine Life Society, Sri Swami Satchidananda (Gurudev to his devotees and students) developed Integral Yoga®. This "is a flexible combination of specific methods designed to develop every aspect of the individual: physical, emotional, intellectual, and spiritual . . . integrating the various branches or paths of yoga in order to bring about this complete and harmonious development." Integral Yoga® classes are based on a sequence of 12 classic postures (with variations) to work every part and system of the body. As well as the postures, deep relaxation, breathing practices, and meditation are used, along with principles of Karma, Bhakti, Jnana, Japa, and Raja yoga to develop an "easeful body, a peaceful mind, and a useful life."

Iyengar Yoga

Founded by B.K.S. Iyengar, Iyengar yoga is one of the more widely known schools of yoga in the West. Often taught as quite a physically demanding style, it emphasizes precise body alignment and attention, or awareness, to detail. Sometimes this may mean spending a whole class going over one posture, or even an aspect of a posture. Iyengar yoga uses blocks and belts to assist the student in attaining a pose.

Kundalini Yoga

Brought to the West in 1969 by Yogi Bhajan, this style concentrates on awakening and releasing the kundalini, or spiritual energy (see chapter 6), which lies dormant at the base of the spine. This style can be very vigorous and taxing for the systems of the body, so make sure that you have an experienced and qualified teacher. Kundalini yoga uses the coordination of classic postures with breathing practices and meditation.

Power Yoga

This new style of yoga is based on, and similar to, Ashtanga yoga.

Sivananda Yoga

Developed by Swami Vishnudevananda, a brother monk of Swami Satchidananda and also a disciple of HH Swami Sivananda. Named after his Master and inspired by his teachings, Sivananda yoga uses five basic principles that can be incorporated into daily life to bring health and happiness. The five principles are proper exercise, breathing, relaxation, positive thinking and meditation, and proper diet.

Viniyoga

Developed by Sri T. Krishnamacharya, who taught B.K.S. Iyengar and K. Pattabhi Jois, Viniyoga uses sequences of postures, incorporating the flow of breath with the movement of the spine. Viniyoga is often taught privately to develop a personal practice for the therapeutic treatment of specific conditions. It includes postures, breathing practices, meditation, study, and reflection.

What Is Yoga?

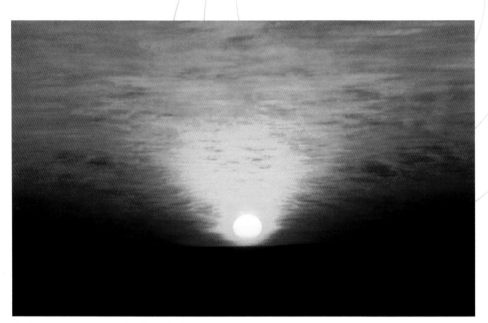

Yogis experiences a sense of unity with all life.

Yoga is a scientific system that combines yoga postures, relaxation, breathing, and meditation techniques with psychological, moral, and ethical principles. Through various combinations of practices determined by temperament and culture (personal preference) the yogi undergoes a complete and harmonious development—physically, emotionally, mentally, and spiritually. Yoga is not a religion. No one is ever told he or she must follow an exact path by only practicing these postures or meditating in this particular way. The student is given suggestions but it is left to the individual to find a path that brings him or her harmony. There are a variety of yogic practices in this book—try the various techniques and principles for yourself and find what works for you.

Most people know that yoga originated in India, but no one knows exactly when. One thing is certain, yoga is not just the latest craze, it has been practiced for thousands of years by people from all walks of life all over the world. Yoga has been proved to bring health to the body, increased vitality and calmness to the mind, and a greater sense of peace and harmony.

Postures

Through the yoga postures, the body undergoes a thorough cleansing, the blood is enriched, and the circulation is improved. Symptoms of old age and stress — tiredness, insomnia, anxiety, general aches and pains, back pain, poor posture, constipation and other digestive disorders, wrinkles, and poor complexion — are greatly reduced and, in some cases, cured. The body begins to develop a younger look and feel. Muscles are toned, and bones and joints are kept flexible and strong.

All the organs of the body are massaged, toned, and flushed with oxygenated blood, which washes away the accumulation of toxins. If you have poor circulation, the body experiences a toxic build up: veins and arteries get blocked; the toxins attack the cells; and the body tissue begins to break down, triggering disease. The toxins from a poor diet, processed and refined foods, alcohol, and smoking are often stored in the body, particularly in the joints. That leads to other degenerative diseases such as rheumatism and arthritis. After doing yoga, many students with these conditions report a significant reduction in their discomfort and improvement in movement; for some students the symptoms disappear completely. The nervous system and all the glands in the body begin to work more effectively, restoring the body's homeostasis, or balance, freeing us from the physical manifestations of stress and depression.

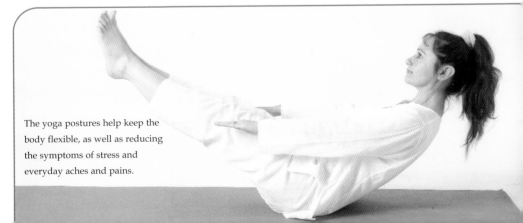

The yoga postures help keep the body flexible, as well as reducing the symptoms of stress and everyday aches and pains.

Breathing

Pranayama improves and strengthens the respiratory system, increasing vitality and energy levels. Many asthma sufferers have experienced significant improvement to their health through regular practice of the breathing techniques. A combination of breathing and deep relaxation has helped many people overcome anxiety and panic attacks. High blood pressure can be significantly decreased and the heart rested. There is now significant research proving that a combination of the various yogic practices can reverse the effects of heart disease and can help in managing and, in some cases, assisting with the cure of some cancers.

The breathing practices in yoga have many beneficial effects.

Concentration and Meditation

Dharana and dhyana will help to free you from mental anxiety, worry, and depression, as you develop feelings of peace and contentment. Students report increased concentration, creativity, clarity of thought, and improved memory.

Suitable for all, yoga brings health and vitality

Yoga and Union

The practices described above are designed to prepare the body and mind for yoga.

The word "yoga" is Sanskrit, an ancient Indian language whose words have more than a literal meaning. The sound and vibration that the words make can have a healing and uplifting effect on the entire system, which is one of the reasons why Sanskrit names for postures are often used in yoga classes. Yoga means to unite or join together. It unites the body, mind, and spirit so that all aspects of the individual function in a harmonious way. The benefits experienced by the practice of the yoga postures, or asanas, help to develop a relaxed and comfortable body. When the body is strong, comfortable, and steady, the breath slows down and the mind becomes calm. When the mind becomes calm, it is freed from mental stress and anxiety, and the yogi begins to experience what can be described as inner peace. The harmony experienced within is extended without, and the yogi begins to experience the world as a more harmonious place.

For a long time, the science of yoga was handed down through the generations by word of mouth from Master to student; there were no books on the subject. The Master or Guru—"the remover of darkness"—instructed the student, who would then practice, practice, practice until the ultimate goal of yoga had been realized; the student, becoming a Master, would then

Yoga balances the body and mind.

continue to pass on the teachings. It was not until Patanjali, the "Father of Yoga," that any instruction on yoga was systematized and written down. Patanjali compiled *The Yoga Sutras*. *Sutra* means "thread." Each sutra gives a brief explanation upon which the Yoga Master expands. Opinion varies greatly as to when the sutras were written.

Estimates range from 5000 BCE to 300 CE. Some Sanskrit scholars believe that they were compiled by a number of Yoga Masters. We will never know the exact truth behind the origins of this ancient Sanskrit text, but *The Yoga Sutras* of Patanjali form the foundation upon which all the various schools of yoga are based.

Control the Mind

Today, many people think of yoga as merely another practice to help them obtain physical perfection. However, Hatha yoga (physical postures) is only a small part of the science of yoga. It was developed as an aid to enable the practitioner to work toward the ultimate goal — the control of the mind.

Patanjali gives us the goal of yoga and how to achieve it in the second sutra of his book:

"Yoga chitta vritti nirodhah" ("the restraint of the modifications of the mind-stuff is yoga").

In other words, if you can control the myriad thoughts that are continually rushing through the mind, affecting you physically and emotionally, you will experience yoga or peace—the union of the body, mind, and spirit. Your true nature is peace, but unfortunately, this peace is disturbed when the mind is distracted. The physical body, through aches, pains, and tension, distracts us. The mind distracts us by trying to fulfil our desires and avoid pain. We begin to think the incessant chattering of the mind is who we really are. "I am happy, I am sad, I am rich, I am a bank manager, I am a

singer, I am fat . . . etc, etc." You are not the mind. You can observe the mind and watch the thoughts coming and going; you are something other than the mind. But the chattering mind forms a cover over our true self. The mind with all its likes and dislikes gets in the way of experiencing our true peaceful nature. To experience this we have to control and still the mind. However, this is incredibly difficult. If it were so easy, there would be lots of enlightened saints and sages walking the planet. My Guru, His Holiness Sri Swami Satchidananda, would say, "It is easier to control a drunk monkey that has been stung by a scorpion than it is to control the mind!"

The ancient Yoga Masters, known as Rishis or Seers, discovered that the mind affects the body. Look at what happens to the body when you have a job interview, when you are going on a first date, when

A clear, still mind reflects the beauty of the true self,
as a still lake reflects the true beauty of nature.

you hear someone close to you has had an accident, or when you are hungry and your dinner is put before you. In addition to affecting the body, what or how you think determines how the world appears to you. What is exciting to one person is stressful or frightening to another. It is not situations and circumstances that are stressful. The way you choose to interpret and respond to the challenges of life is what causes stress. The way you choose to respond to various situations is determined by your past experiences, parents, culture, religion, etc. The world itself is a reflection of the individual mind.

Imagine a clear, still lake in the middle of the mountains, reflecting perfectly the world around. Throw a stone into the lake and ripples are formed; a breeze comes up, and the lake becomes choppy, sand and mud are disturbed, and the water is no longer clear. The reflection of the world is distorted.

When the mind is controlled and still, it reflects your true peaceful self within. Thoughts, emotions, and desires are like the ripples caused when a stone is thrown into the lake; emotional upsets disturb the pure mind. They color the mind, covering the light within, and distort your view of yourself and the world around.

The Seers reasoned that if the mind affected how they viewed the world and the body, then through control of the body, they could control the mind and have a more positive outlook on life. They discovered that the breath was the interconnection between the body and mind. Have you noticed that when you are upset or agitated, the breath is rapid, short, and uneven? When you are relaxed and calm the breath becomes slow, deep, and even. When you are fully concentrated on one thing, the breath practically stops and you find yourself having to take a gasp of air; the breath is reflecting the state of the body and mind. If you can keep the body still, the breath will slow down and

It is not always easy to sit still and control your mind. You can become very aware of any aches or pains, and your mind can begin whirring with a melee of thoughts.

eventually, after a lot of complaining, the mind will calm down.

However, it's not that easy to keep the body still, particularly if it's full of toxins and tension. Try and sit still for five minutes. Before you know it, a long list of desires and complaints are racing through the mind, "My back aches, my hips hurt, I want a drink, I must make that phone call, I want something to eat, etc. . ." How long before you give in to the demands of the senses and mind? Before you know it, your peace of mind gets disturbed; what's more, your peace of mind will not be restored until your desires have been fulfilled. However, once fulfilled, it won't be long before another desire pops up to agitate the mind. So how can you get some control over the senses and mind?

All the yogic practices, including Hatha yoga, are designed to help the yogi gain control over the body, breath, senses, and mind. This control leads to permanent peace, joy, and unconditional love—a higher level of consciousness that has been given different names, including enlightenment, cosmic consciousness, higher consciousness, self-realization, and nirvana. Through yoga you can find your way back to this peaceful, blissful place.

It is often difficult to free your mind from everyday thoughts.

Contentment, Happiness— Permanent Peace and Joy

All humans search for lasting happiness and contentment. The way in which this is fulfilled will vary according to individual development. Unfortunately, most of us try to find this happiness in a world of constant change, where nothing is permanent; therefore, the happiness we experience is transitory. So we find ourselves caught up in a game of chasing our tails, never really getting what we want—permanent happiness. Instead, we find temporary happiness, with unhappiness just around the corner.

Reality Versus Illusion

Humans have a tendency always to look for the next best thing to make them happy; running after something new, whether it's a car, house, dress, relationship, or job; chasing the illusion of happiness.

According to yogic philosophy, what we consider to be real is in fact illusory. How can we say that the world we experience is real when no two experiences of the world are the same and when what we experience ourselves is always changing? What is pleasant and pleasing to you might be upsetting to me. Who is right? What is real? Even if we both agree that the sunset is beautiful, we experience it differently.

People are always chasing happiness, often thinking it comes from material possessions. Yoga challenges this view of happiness.

Your new partner might be the most beautiful person in the world to you, while everyone else wonders what you see in him or her. How you experience the world is a reflection of your mind and that reflection changes from one minute to the next. In a couple of years, or maybe weeks, your wonderful new partner might seem to be the meanest and most selfish person you have come across. Your mother, on the other hand, has grown to like your partner after that wonderful birthday present she was given! How you experience the world and the people in it (what you call reality) is based on your mind, and your mind is nothing more than a bundle of thoughts, which are continually changing. The clothes you wore when you were younger when you thought you looked so cool and trendy only make kids laugh and you cringe. Did the clothes change? No. But the way you think about them did. Everything in the manifest universe is continually changing, and if we look outside ourselves for happiness, fulfilment, and reality, we are always going to be disappointed because the happiness and reality that the world brings us is temporary, always changing, and therefore not real.

You cannot know what my experience of a sunset feels like to me. I cannot know what your experience feels like. Which one is real? "They are both real," you might say. If that is the case, then we have two realities, which by definition is not real!

From Diversity to Unity

Many people go about their daily lives in a self-centered way.
Egotistically putting themselves first, trying to fulfill personal desires
and avoid pain in whatever form it manifests itself.

By living in a self-centered way, we become distant from each other. We further reduce our sense of relatedness by continually judging, comparing, and criticizing our fellow beings. The more we judge and then label or categorize each other, the more petty differences and separation we create. If you judge people from a self-centered point of view, you will usually find a negative category to place them in. The ego always looks for a way to put itself first and to be better than the next guy. As nice a person as you might be, your instinctive drive for survival will make you behave in this way to some extent, unless you begin to develop a higher awareness of what is going on. Many people go about their daily lives in a self-centered way. Egotistically putting themselves first, trying to fulfil personal desires and avoid pain in whatever form it manifests itself.

Yoga teaches us that we are all inextricably linked. Modern science now

agrees with what the Rishis realized through deep states of meditation; at our most fundamental level we are all nothing but energy; there is nothing but energy of which we are a part—we are all One. There is no difference between us. The differences we

As young children, we are rarely bothered by differences. It is only as we get older that we are liable to judge other people. Yoga teaches us that we are all linked.

Yoga helps us to recognize that we are at one with nature.

experience are a figment of our imagination. Through the practice of yoga, we can begin to remove the "veil of illusion" or "maya" (see chapter 5, pages 137–158) that prevents us from seeing our "true self." This illusion prevents us from experiencing a deep sense of peace and of being at one with ourselves and with the universe. For the yogi this is the goal of life.

Within each of us is a divine spark, the individual spirit, or *atman*. However, we have forgotten our divine nature because we identify with the mind and our ego-dominated self. All the different experiences that life brings us, whether we call them good or bad, whether they make us happy or sad, are lessons to help us to evolve. As we evolve, we grow closer to realizing our true nature and to becoming one with the universal divine energy, or spirit, which in yoga is called Brahman. It is like a wave rising up and thinking it's the whole ocean, only to realize it is simply part of a whole as it becomes one with the ocean once again. As Swami Satchidananda put it—the goal of yoga is to "realize the spiritual unity behind the diversity found in nature."

3

Paths of Yoga

People are different—what suits one may not suit another. Yoga works with this diversity.

To realize and experience our true nature, we need to be able to control the mind, humble the ego, and rise above our lower nature. In this chapter, we look at the different paths of yoga to gain an understanding of the various ways in which this control can be mastered. People have many different moods and temperaments

and come from different cultural backgrounds—what helps the fisherman from Gambia experience peace is not necessarily going to help a financial consultant from the City of London, and what helps him might not help a housewife from Romania. One of the reasons why yoga has stood the test of time is that it takes this diversity into consideration.

Dedication to the practices from any one, or a combination, of the six paths of yoga will bring peace, helping you to gain and maintain your health and happiness. Don't worry if you don't like some of the practices or if you don't agree with some of the philosophy. Try the practices; apply the philosophy—if you still don't like them, that's fine. It's a bit like trying on a jacket in a store—if it fits well and feels comfortable, take it home and use it, if not leave it at the store.

Karma Yoga: The Path of Action

Karma is the natural law of cause and effect; the concept that every action has a reaction and that you will eventually end up reaping what you have sown, whether good or bad. It is important to realize that this is not because the universe, God, nature, your higher self (call it what you will) wants to punish you. Experiences, good or bad, are lessons helping us to learn from our mistakes. Unfortunately for us, or fortunately if we look at this with the right understanding, we seem to learn more quickly from painful experiences.

Experiences, good and bad, can teach us valuable lessons. Understanding this is one of the key elements of yoga, and helps ease negative feelings.

Understanding the law of karma can help us to accept difficult or upsetting situations. The karma yogi welcomes the pain that life can and will bring and sees it as a blessing, an opportunity to grow. If someone upsets you, instead of trying to get even or making yourself depressed by dwelling on how unfair life is, accept that you must have done something in the past to upset someone and it is only now that you are having to pay for that action. Sometimes it seems that the innocent get hurt but karma is not always instant— maybe the innocent person today was a sinner last week, or 10 years ago or in a past life.

Always a little controversial, yoga philosophy includes the concept of reincarnation. Until all the karma is worked out, a soul will continue to take birth after birth. Each lifetime will give the necessary experiences to work off the karmic debt. However, as well as working off the karmic debt, we also create new karma and so enter the endless cycle of birth, death, and rebirth unless we learn to control the mind and attain enlightenment. The only way to wipe the slate clean of your negative karma and to avoid accumulating more is to engage yourself in selfless service. By engaging in selfless service you are performing Karma yoga.

Anyone can practice yoga—anywhere and at any time.

"The definition of yoga is perfection in action. Whatever you do—your thoughts, words and deeds—let there be perfection. What is a perfect act? One that brings some benefit to somebody and no harm to anybody. The reward of service is the joy of having served. When you have that joy, the mind is always calm and serene."

Sri Swami Satchidananda

This is the essence of Karma yoga. Do whatever you can to the best of your ability, without expectation of reward, concern for criticism, or thought of the outcome.

Karma yoga can be practiced by anyone at any time. It is a great path for those who are very active and find it hard to sit still— meditation for people of an active nature may bring more pain than peace. It is worth

Yoga encourages selflessness, and doing things for others.

pointing out that we are not just talking about physical action. All physical action is a manifestation of thought. Watch your mind, the never-ending mental activity. When you take up Karma yoga, there is no drastic change on the outside, although people close to you may notice that you approach your work with more joy and care and with more thought for others. The transformation that occurs through practicing Karma yoga is internal. You will no longer experience the anxiety that comes with being attached to the outcome of your work—embarrassment when things go wrong; fear; nervousness worrying whether or not things will work out right; pride when you get praise; disappointment when you don't get the praise you think you deserve. Through Karma yoga, you can use physical activity

to control mental activity; you can calm down all the unnecessary chatter and free your mind from troubling thoughts.

When practicing Karma yoga, keep the mind focused on the job at hand, not allowing it to wander aimlessly. If you keep the mind focused, you cannot worry about the outcome or make yourself miserable wishing you were somewhere else. Have you ever had the experience of returning home in the car and not remembering the journey? Your mind has been so engaged in the past or future that the present has passed by unnoticed. The karma yogi doesn't get bored or think that he is too good for a particular job. All work great or small is of equal importance. No one is inferior or superior; everyone is treated with respect and love.

The karma yogi does not take the credit or praise from a job well done; she knows that the identification with the fruits of her action will bring unhappiness later on. Karma yoga is selfless service, perfection in action. Doing things for others and not for yourself. A perfect act is one that does not hurt anyone and benefits at least one other. Through selfless service, you can purify the ego. This will enable you to serve even better and also to become more sensitive to other people as you will be thinking of benefiting them and not yourself. The goal is to transcend the individual self, to become an instrument in the hands of the Divine; with this realization, you become one with the Divine.

The karma yogi does his best and leaves the rest. With no fear, anxiety, or expectations for the results of his actions, work becomes joyful.

life seems easy; it's like a blessing from God. Energy will flow through you and you will be of much service. It doesn't matter what your dharma is. There is no inferior

"There is no individual doer of any action; all action is a Divine happening through a human object."

Belkash Ramlikar

If you find your work is continually causing you grief in one way or another and disturbing your peace, it might be worth looking for something more fulfilling. What would make you want to get out of bed in the morning? What is your dharma, your duty to the world? When you discover what it is that you are naturally predisposed to do,

or superior work—everyone and everything is needed.

Remember—the goal of yoga is to calm and transcend the mind to experience peace. Keeping the mind fully engaged in what you are doing and not being concerned for the fruits of the outcome will significantly reduce your thoughts.

Bhakti Yoga:
The Path of Devotion

Bhakti yoga is great for people of a devotional and/or emotional nature. To practice Bhakti yoga all that is required is love. The bhakti yogi sees everyone and everything as God and performs all actions as an offering to God. To love God as formless, nameless, absolute is particularly difficult for the finite mind. The bhakti yogi will choose a particular aspect of the Divine and concentrate fully upon that, directing constant love, thought, devotion, and service to God, a particular Divine incarnation, or the spiritual teacher or Guru. Whether your God is Allah, Moses, Christ, Nature, or Krishna, it doesn't matter. If God is absolute, omniscient, omnipotent, and omnipresent, then God is all these and more, so it doesn't matter what aspect of the Divine you pick.

In daily life the bhakti yogi will constantly remind themselves of God. They will surround themselves with pictures or objects to help bring the mind back to God. They will read holy scriptures or writings from saints and sages. They will pray and chant mantras or repeat the name of God. The bhakti will practice kirtan, or the singing and chanting of Divine names. Bhakti yogis are also karma yogis; they offer all that they do and all they receive to God. Pleasure or pain comes from God and the bhakti offers it back to God. The bhakti will develop a personal relationship with their chosen deity or aspect of God—talking to him as if to a friend, child, or servant. They feel that God is always watching over them and guiding them in all that they do. Eventually prayer isn't necessary as God is seen in everything and everyone and the bhakti experiences unconditional love for the whole of creation.

The bhakti totally surrenders his individual will to God's will—"All is thine, I am thine, Thy will be done"—and sees himself as a

vehicle for the Divine grace to function through. However, you don't have to worship a particular religious aspect of God or a spiritual teacher to be a bhakti. To love your mother and father or your children unconditionally, to serve them selflessly, to see the Divine in them (which can be really challenging sometimes!) is to be a bhakti yogi. To treat all your possessions and all objects with love and care, to be kind and gentle to all living things is to be a bhakti. If you want to experience God or inner peace, learn to love everything unconditionally, with no expectations or conditions.

Just love and serve. Through love transcend all the differences of the petty lower nature and realize your true self.

Whatever creed the bhakti yogi follows, God will always be at the forefront of their mind.

Jnana Yoga:
The Path of Wisdom

Perhaps one of the more difficult paths, Jnana yoga is for people of a more intellectual tendency, who have a reflective mind and an analytical nature. Jnana yoga is a more direct approach to realizing one's true nature. Whatever action the jnana yogi engages in, she always strives to maintain the awareness that she is not the doer of any action. She does not consider herself to be the body or the mind; she has a body and mind and is a silent witness of what is going on with both. Striving to identify with the part of the mind that is watching the action rather than the part that is engaged with the action, the jnani will develop the thought, "I'm not working, nature is working through me." The jnani is not bound by work or any action; all experience is seen as something to learn from. As well as being a jnana yogi she would also practice Karma yoga but from a jnana rather than a bhakti viewpoint.

The jnani wouldn't say, "I'm working hard and I'm tired." The jnani would observe that there was tiredness in the body because it had been engaged in hard work. The two attitudes actually make a huge difference to how you feel. As we have already seen, the thoughts affect the body—if you say, "I'm tired" or "I'm in pain" that is what you create. When you observe or witness what is going on, that is the end of it. You don't instigate a chain reaction of thoughts and emotions, which then affect your whole day. Observe, acknowledge, and move on, maintaining a peaceful mind. The jnani detaches herself from the situation and is not identified with the action, thought, or emotion, for none of this is real, her true self is something beyond this.

Our true nature is to be peaceful and blissful. It's not that we have to become

To dwell on one negative thought will start a chain reaction that leads to stress, worry, or depression. Learn to observe thoughts; watch them come and go like the passing of clouds. You are not your thoughts.

enlightened—we already are—but due to false identification with the thoughts, or to be more precise with the thought of "I am . . . (fill in the gap!)," we hide our true self. The jnani approach is to negate everything that we are not, which gets in the way of realizing our true nature. This is called the "neti-neti" method. It means "not this, not this." If you feel upset ask yourself, "Who is upset?" There are thoughts in the mind, which are disturbing, but that is all they are—thoughts that will soon disappear if you observe them and let them go. The true self cannot be anything that is perceived through the senses or conceived by the mind. All these things are impermanent and therefore not real. To be real, by definition, is to be permanent; therefore the systematic intellectual removal of all that is not real will eventually lead to what is real. The "veil of illusion," or maya, will be removed and the true self revealed. One of my teachers once said, "it is not that we are human trying to be divine; but rather we are divine trying to learn how to be human," so we can live in a way that reflects our true self.

Japa Yoga: The Path of Mantra Repetition

Although often seen as part of Bhakti yoga, this is a path that leads to control of the mind in and of itself. Japa is also of benefit to the karma and jnana yogi as it helps to prevent the mind from wandering. Japa yoga uses the repetition of mantras, or sound vibrations, to transcend the chattering mind. In deep meditative states the Rishis experienced subtle sound vibrations, which they formulated into mantras for repetition. The meaning of the mantra is not important; mantras are sound vibrations made up of one or more syllables that represent a particular aspect of the Divine. Through concentrated repetition of the mantra, its vibrations permeate the individual's entire system, bringing health to the body and calming the senses and mind, making them fit to handle the challenges of life. The vibrations created by mantra repetition gently cleanse all the cells in the body. This practice is also very calming for the nerves and emotions. The mind is concentrated and elevated, eventually bringing spiritual awareness.

The universe is energy; the energy vibrates and the vibration makes a sound or a hum. In Sanskrit, this hum is produced by chanting "Om" (ahh ooo mmmm—aum—making the "m" long and feeling the resonance in the head). Sound vibrations create forms. The hum of the universe is the basis for everything else. Everything, including humans, is made up of sound vibrations. When we repeat mantras, we change our vibration and align, or tune, our self into the hum of the universe.

If you are depressed or angry, you will have a particular vibration or energy about you. I am sure you have walked into a room and sensed that your friends have just been arguing, even though they are smiling at you. If you have ever had the good fortune to be in the presence of a holy person, you will feel peaceful, even if they haven't spoken, because that is the vibration they emanate and you can tune into that. In the same way that you tune your radio to pick up different radio waves, we can tune our selves to receive divine energy waves. Notice how you feel when you listen to heavy metal music or punk rock compared to when you listen to a Mozart violin concerto or music for deep relaxation. Sound vibrations affect every cell in your body and thus affect how you feel emotionally and mentally. Japa can even

waking state

transcendental state

"veil of illusion" — maya

dream state

deep, dreamless sleep

The symbol for Om: the primordial sound or hum of the universe. When the yogi transcends the lower nature of the mind, passing through the veil of illusion, he then rests in the transcendental state of Samadhi.

influence an atmosphere or a place. You could say that mantra repetition helps to protect you from picking up negative waves of energy; keep repeating your mantra and you will attract positive energy.

To practice Japa yoga, you may have a particular time of the day when you sit and repeat your mantra. However, the aim is to keep the mantra going throughout the day. Use the mind when you need to work and at all other times repeat your mantra. At first it is unlikely that you will have the mental control to do this. You might remember every so often and then the mind will be off. However, stick with it. As you repeat your mantra, many thoughts will pop up; gradually, as you gain control over the mind, you will be able to keep focused upon the mantra and disturbing thoughts will lose their grip (see chapter 7).

Repetition of a mantra is a great way to calm down and gain control over the mind, helping you to feel peaceful.

Hatha Yoga: The Path of Physical Perfection

Hatha yoga is mainly concerned with the development of the physical body through asanas (postures), yoga nidra (deep relaxation), pranayama (breath control), and diet. (See chapters 4, 5, 6, and 8.)

You could say that Hatha yoga is meditation of the physical body. The asanas, pranayama, etc. must be performed with consciousness otherwise it is not yoga; the body, breath, and mind must be working in harmony with each other. The sign of an advanced hatha yogi is the one who can keep the mind fully focused on the breath and body at all times, regardless of the asana being held. The beginner is the one whose mind is wandering all over the place without awareness of what the breath and body are doing. Even if you can stand on your head for an hour, if the mind and breath are not harmonized, you are still a beginner.

There is no difference between the body and mind. The body is a gross manifestation of the mind, and the mind a subtle manifestation of the body. They are inextricably linked, and the breath is the connection between them. Physical upset or illness will affect the mind, and disturbing thoughts will affect the body. Through Hatha yoga harmony or balance can be brought to the whole being. In *The Yoga Sutras*, Patanjali says, "Sthira sukham asanam" ("Asana is a steady, comfortable posture"). Any posture that brings steadiness and comfort is an asana. When the body is steady and comfortable, we can sit still and calm the mind. For most of us the body is filled with tension and toxins, which makes it very difficult to keep it either steady or comfortable. As soon as you try to keep a steady pose, the body and mind will complain.

Ha equals sun and relates to the positive energy, masculine, heat, rational, logical, assertive aspects of our nature, while *tha* equals moon and relates to the negative energy, feminine, creative, intuitive, relaxed aspects. When we practice Hatha yoga correctly, there will be a balance and a joining of these two subtle sides of our being. So we need to get the balance right—not so much strain that it causes suffering, but not so lazy that there is no work being done at all.

When practiced correctly Hatha yoga brings balance and health to all the systems of the body. General physical exercise works the muscular, skeletal, and cardiovascular systems. However, if your endocrine or nervous system is weak or out of balance your exercise could put extra stress on them, which in turn will affect your overall physical, mental, and emotional health. The systems of the body are not designed to sit still all day and then burst into vigorous activity; this puts too much stress on the body. An airplane wing is designed to deal with a certain amount of tension; it enables the plane to take off and

Constantly juggling too many commitments can lead to stress.

Blood pressure can soar when under stress or threat.

fly properly. However, if the tension becomes too great it turns into stress, and the wing of the plane can break up. In the same way, a little tension keeps us motivated and tones the muscles, but too much stresses the body, which will also break down.

The nervous system is the control and communications system for the entire body and mind. It is responsible for the overall balance, or homeostasis, of the body, mind, and emotions. It controls sensations and actions, monitors changes in all parts of the body, and is responsible for our thoughts and memory. Messages from the outside world are picked up through the senses, or sense receptors—the skin, ears, eyes, and nose—and sent via a network of nerves to the brain. Responding to what is going on, within and without the body, the nervous system will interpret changes and send an electrical pulse to activate a particular muscle or give a message to a particular gland to secrete hormones.

The endocrine system is also responsible for maintaining homeostasis and works in conjunction with the nervous system. The electrical impulses released from the nervous system are quick, short-lived messages, whereas the endocrine system releases chemicals or hormones into the blood stream slowly, and the effects are much longer lasting. When the nervous and endocrine systems function in harmony, physical, mental, and emotional health is maintained, and you will respond in a positive way to all the challenges of life. If, however, the balance is distorted, these two systems will continually send out messages to prepare the body for an emergency and will overreact to stressful situations.

When the body feels under threat, the sympathetic nervous system springs into action and increases the heartbeat and

We often turn to things that are bad for us when under stress.

blood pressure; the bronchioles in the lungs dilate, the urinary and digestive systems shut down, and the body is pumped with adrenaline and noradrenaline. The body and mind are preparing for "fight or flight."

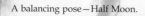

A balancing pose—Half Moon.

exhaustion. When the endocrine system is unbalanced, the metabolism is affected in a negative way, which can lead to obesity, menstrual disorders and, in some cases, serious disease.

Through Hatha yoga postures the nervous, endocrine, and digestive systems are cleansed and strengthened. This, in turn, works the cardiovascular system and you will find that the muscles are toned and the bones and joints strengthened. Hatha yoga calms the body, homeostasis is returned and all the systems are energized and revitalized.

Whether the threat is emotional, mental, or physical, in a balanced body the parasympathetic nervous system will switch on and turn off the stress response, allowing the body to relax. The parasympathetic system also ensures the correct functioning of digestion and elimination.

However, in modern society, the sympathetic nervous system is continually stimulated. When out of balance the "fight or flight" switch stays on; this leads to chronic fatigue, hypertension, depression, anxiety, and nervous disorders. Often the way we cope with these feelings is to have a cup of coffee or a chocolate bar. The chemical lift is only temporary, and stimulants of this kind ultimately put more stress on the functioning of the body and add to the symptoms of stress and

The spine is literally the backbone of our health. The spinal cord is our lifeline, and when we are in balance, energy flows up and down it, bringing vitality. The Hatha yoga postures bend and twist the spine, literally cutting through the physical manifestations of stress—energy in the spine is released, and we feel revitalized.

Today we have cures for many diseases that would have been fatal not so long ago, but we are still left with degenerative disease, all of which can be traced back to stress of the body, mind, and emotions. The practice of Hatha yoga brings us back to a place of ease, balance, harmony, and peace.

Raja Yoga: The Royal Path

The *Yoga Sutras* (see chapter 2) was the first "handbook" on Raja yoga. The sutras give us a systematic guide on how to control the mind, the obstacles that may prevent us gaining this control, how to overcome them, and the results one can experience through following the steps of Raja yoga.

Raja yoga is concerned with control of the mind through the development of all aspects of the individual. Beginning with moral and ethical perfection, leading to the practice of concentration and meditation and culminating in the final goal of yoga—union with the Divine—samadhi.

This path deals with the mind directly and is known as the "royal" or "kingly" yoga, as raja means king. This practice is also known as Ashtanga yoga (not to be confused with the style of yoga called Ashtanga—see chapter 1). Ashtanga means eight-fold. There are eight steps or limbs to systematically work through before attaining samadhi. This is a great path for anyone who is interested in the mind and learning how it works. What you discover with Raja yoga is that it encompasses all the other paths of yoga—another reason why it is know as the "kingly path."

The eight steps of raja yoga

1. Yamas (restraints)

Ahimsa	Harmlessness
Satya	Truthfulness
Asteya	Non-stealing
Brahmacharya	Continence or Moderation
Aparigraha	Non-greed

2. Niyama (observances)

Saucha	Purity
Samtosha	Contentment
Tapas	Austerity (receiving but not causing pain)
Svadhyaya	Spiritual study
Ishwarapranidhana	Surrender to the Lord

3. Asana (physical postures)

4. Pranayama (breath control)

5. Pratyahara (sense withdrawal or controlling the senses)

6. Dharana (concentration)

7. Dhyana (meditation)

8. Samadhi (contemplation, absorption, or super-conscious state)

The practice of Raja yoga can enhance all physical and mental abilities. To make sure that the "super human" puts his abilities to good use, Raja yoga begins with moral and ethical development. Yamas and niyama are concerned with the way we treat ourselves and the world around us. They are the yogic "dos and don'ts" that enhance the quality of life for everyone. You will find similar codes of conduct in the ten commandments of the Christian and Jewish faiths, as well as in the ten virtues of Buddhism. All religions and spiritual paths have a moral code that forms the basis of human behavior upon which a loving society can be built (if only we would all put these codes into practice!). It is worth pointing out that the yamas and niyamas are a means to achieving the goal of yoga and not the goal in themselves. However, the practice and understanding of the first two steps make the other six much easier (see chapter 9).

The eight limbs of Raja yoga are practiced simultaneously—it would take several lifetimes to perfect each step before moving on to the next! Samadhi is the culmination of all the other limbs. Raja yoga helps us to remove our physical and mental impurities so that our true self shines brightly.

Raja yoga goes far beyond a "do good" and "be good" moral practice. It leads the practitioner step by step to a deep understanding and experience of the true nature of the mind, which in turn leads him to experience his true self. To achieve this, the raja yogi does not depend on an external object of devotion as in Bhakti yoga. Self-realization is achieved through self-discipline and the effort to peel away the layers of the mind.

4

Hatha Yoga
(Physical Postures)

Preparing for Your Practice

- Be sure to check with your doctor or health care professional if you are recovering from a recent operation, illness, or injury before starting to practice Hatha yoga. If you have any condition for which you take medication, it is also best to seek advice before trying the postures in this section.

- Do not practice Hatha yoga if you are up to 13 weeks pregnant unless you have had a regular hatha practice for some time. If you are over 13 weeks pregnant, find a teacher who specializes in prenatal yoga.

- If you are menstruating it is best to avoid inverted postures. You don't want to go against the flow of nature and inverting the body, in some cases, can cause flooding. It is also a good idea to avoid anything that causes too much pressure on the abdominal area. During menstruation it is better to do more relaxation, gentle breathing practices, and meditation. Try to rest, nurture, and revitalize yourself during this time.

- Don't eat for at least 2–3 hours before a class. It can be uncomfortable to practice the postures on a full stomach and may even make you feel sick. Practicing the postures also interrupts digestion, which can cause indigestion. Drinking water before the class will aid the elimination process. If you have problems with blood sugar levels you can have some soft fruit or fruit juice an hour before class.

- If possible try not to eat for an hour after the class. This allows the body to carry on with the elimination of toxins. If you have something to eat, elimination stops and digestion begins.

- Wear loose, comfortable clothing. It's better to wear natural fibers, as these will absorb sweat and toxins released during the postures and allow the skin to breathe. If you get cold feet, wear socks but no special footwear is required.

- It's best to remove jewelry as it can get caught or dig into the body and generally gets in the way.

- It's a good idea to remove hard contact lenses as they may pop out. Soft lenses are fine.

- Use a folded blanket, camping or exercise mat to practice your postures on. Make sure you are going to be comfortable, particularly when lying on your front—the hipbones have a tendency to dig into the floor and a little padding can make all the difference. Non-slip yoga mats are particularly useful for standing poses but you may need some extra padding when you lie down. You want to be able to keep a steady posture in order to quieten the mind; this is particularly difficult if it is complaining about being uncomfortable!

- You may find a pillow or cushion makes it easier to sit and lie on the floor.

- If practicing at home, try to do your Hatha yoga session at the same time each day so that you can build a regular routine. First thing in the morning or last thing at night are good times. The morning is a great time of day to practice your Hatha yoga before the mind gets too busy. It may suit you best to practice in the evening when all the jobs for the day have been done. Pick a time of day that is going to work for you. A time when you won't be disturbed either by the phone or by your mind reminding you of all the things you have to do. This is your time for you to take care of yourself, physically, emotionally, and mentally.

- If you are practicing in the morning, the body will usually be a little stiff. Start slowly and give the body a chance to warm up.

Performing the Postures

- Do not force or strain in any of the postures.

- If you feel uncomfortable, at any time, come out of the pose and rest. Don't wait until you feel pain!

- Keep the breath easy. If you find that you are holding or laboring the breath, then you are probably straining the body. If you are straining the body, you will be disturbing the mind—come out of the pose and rest. Remember you want to revitalize the body, not exhaust it!

- Learn to keep a positive conversation about the body. We often judge and criticize ourselves in a negative way. "I can't do this," "I'm no good at that," "I hate my . . ." etc. As you think so you become. Talk encouragingly and lovingly to yourself, nurture the body. If you find a pose particularly difficult, visualize yourself in a more advanced position. Every cell in the body will react to the images and thoughts in the mind so "cultivate divine thoughts" (Swami Sivananda).

- Accept yourself as you are. If you want to change anything in life, you must first accept what is so. It doesn't matter how far you bend or stretch in any of the postures. Yoga is not competitive; learn to work to your own ability. Whatever you are doing, whatever your ability, the balanced sequences of postures in this book will bring benefit to your body, emotions, and mind.

- Relax into the postures. Always check to see if you are tensing anything unnecessarily. The more you relax, the more the body will naturally stretch.

- If you perform short, quick, jerky movements, the body will tense, you won't stretch so far, and you are likely to strain or injure yourself.

- As you relax into the postures, you will release tension in the body. As you release physical tension, you will release mental tension, freeing yourself from the buildup of stress and anxiety.

- Have the eyes closed as much as possible. This brings the focus inward and helps to stop the mind from being distracted.

- Try to keep the mind or awareness focused on the body or breath. Notice which parts of the body are working. Where are you feeling the pose most? On an exhalation tell that part of the body to "let go" or "relax."

Yoga is not competitive. It is beneficial regardless of how far you can stretch!

The Asanas in This Book

When thinking about the asanas, or postures, to include in this book, I decided to give you a balanced Hatha yoga session that would work all parts and systems of the body. This is the basic Hatha yoga Level 1 Class as taught by Integral Yoga®. The session is made up of 12 classic asanas, plus some variations either to add to your session or to use as variations. Once you have become familiar with the sequence, you will be able to move from one posture to the next while keeping the breath and mind focused on what you are doing. In that way the session will become a moving meditation. You can then add a deep relaxation, breathing practices, and a brief meditation for your overall health and well-being.

If you decide to go to a yoga class, you will have a good grounding in some of the more popular and beneficial postures.

Rather than doing lots of different postures, it is much better to do a few, do them well, and hold them for longer. An asana is a firm and steady posture. Do not exceed the timings given for each pose until you can hold the pose steady, comfortably, and mindfully. Then, gradually begin to increase the time of

holding. When you hold the poses, the benefits are increased and the mind calms down and becomes more concentrated.

Always wanting to do new and different poses is a continuation of always looking for something new or better to make you happy, instead of learning to be content with what you have. Happiness comes from within. Feeling good comes from within. Don't always be looking for something new. Increase the length of time you hold the postures and begin to experience a peaceful, calm mind that comes from turning the awareness inward.

An advanced hatha yogi will practice fewer poses, will hold them steady for longer, and will keep the mind focused.

Yoga is not about gymnastics or showing off. There is no need to be competitive, not even with yourself. Work to your own ability, accepting and being content with whatever that is. And know that whatever postures you do, you are bringing great benefit to your body, energy levels, emotions, mind, and spirit.

The postures are divided into six sections: warm up, standing poses, backward bending poses, forward bending poses, inverted poses, rotated poses—and one last final posture.

The classic session of 12 postures would be: Netra Vyaayaamam (Eye Movements), Surya Namaskaram (Sun Worship), Bhujangasana (Cobra Pose), Ardha Salabasana (Half Locust Pose), Salabasana (Locust Pose), Dhanurasana (Bow Pose), Janursirshasana (Head to Knee Pose), Paschimottanasana (Full Forward Bend), Sarvangasana (Shoulder Stand), Matsyasana (Fish Pose), Ardha Matsyendrasana (Half Spinal Twist), and Yoga Mudra (Yogic Seal).

Making Up Your Own Session

- Once you know the postures, and depending on how long you hold them, this sequence will take 30–45 minutes. As you begin to hold poses for longer, do fewer poses. Adjust the sequence and times to suit your needs.

- If you only have time for a short session, make sure it is balanced. Warm up, do a back bend, a forward bend and a twist, or a back bend, forward bend and an inverted posture. Always end with Yoga Mudra to calm the mind and to bring the awareness within.

- You can add one or two standing poses after the Sun Worship or after the twisting section.

- If you are doing a longer session, make sure you take a moment to rest between the postures and a slightly longer rest between the different sections.

Developing a Practice

If you would like to have a regular practice but find it hard to discipline yourself, start out by practicing just one posture a day. Do the one pose every day, preferably at the same time. If you say to yourself, "I'm going to do an hour or half an hour a day," the mind can always think of lots of other things you need to do. No matter how good your intentions, you never seem to have the time. To build a regular habit, start with something that is achievable. Once you regularly do your one posture, you can begin to add others. What students generally find is that if they do their one pose, it feels so good that they do one more, then one more . . . But the trick is to tell the mind you are only going to do one. Treat the mind like a little child. Be firm and loving. Do you remember being told or saying, "just one more spoonful"?

Observing the Postures

If you find some of these poses challenging to begin with, try the alternatives or modifications. There is no hurry. Take your time to discover how the body feels and responds to the various postures. Notice how they make you feel mentally and emotionally. We can sometimes learn a lot about ourselves by noticing how we react to certain postures.

The body is a reflection of the mind. Yoga teaches us to understand the body, leading to a greater understanding of the mind. Release tension from the body and release tension and anxiety from the mind. Develop a flexible body and enjoy the development of a flexible mind, a mind that can adapt, adjust, and accommodate different people and changing situations with ease. They say that stiffness in the body reflects stiffness in the mind, a lack of ability to accept change. Apparently, when you are dead the body can be folded in half—the chest on the thighs! As my Master, Sri Swami Satchidananda, would say, "all's well that bends well!"

I had a student who was agoraphobic and suffered severe panic attacks when she left the house. I taught her for several years,

visiting her at her home. She really didn't like the Sun Worship or the standing postures. She practiced regularly between our lessons but would often "forget" to practice this warm-up sequence. During one particular lesson, we talked about what it was that she didn't like about the sequence. Was it uncomfortable? Did she find it difficult? She suddenly realized that the postures made her feel energized and confident—feelings that were new and that she didn't feel comfortable with. She was used to

being afraid and staying at home. Although unpleasant, this was normal and her survival had become based on these negative feelings. Noticing how she felt, acknowledging and accepting her feelings, and then making herself work with these postures, deep breathing and affirmation transformed her life. She phoned me one day to say that she had been to the supermarket on her own. Within a couple of months, she was reading the week's lesson at her local church—something she never thought in a million years she would be able to do.

Warming Up the Body and Focusing the Mind

Before you begin your session, take a few moments to sit quietly and allow the mind to calm down. Leave behind all the stresses and strains of the day if you are practicing in the evening. Focus your awareness in the present moment.

Sit in a comfortable seated position— either crossed-legged or kneeling.

Before You Start

Make sure you read all the instructions and modifications for a pose before you try it out. Try to see how the pose is performed in the mind's eye before you attempt the posture for the first time.

Two more things—have fun and smile!

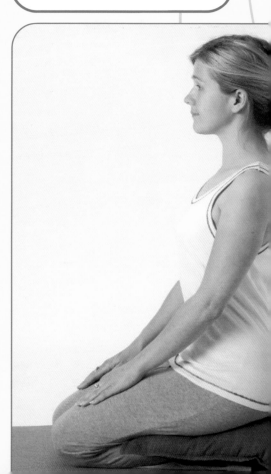

Meditative Poses — Sitting Postures

Sukhasana (Comfortable Pose)

Simply cross both feet under the thighs . . .

.

. . . or sit with the ankles uncrossed, one leg placed in front of the other.

Ardha Padmasana (Half Lotus)

1

Sit with both legs extended.

2

Bend the right knee and bring it up toward the chest.

Caution: If there is any discomfort in the knees and hips, return to Sukhasana.

3

Now let the knee drop to the side.

4

Wrap the right arm over the leg and take hold of the calf. With the left hand, take hold of the ankle, cradling the leg.

5

Gently place the top of the right foot on the left thigh and relax the knee down toward the floor.

6

If this is comfortable, bend the left leg and place the foot under the right thigh.

Variations

- If you find it difficult to sit on the floor keeping the spine erect, try sitting on the edge of a cushion. This helps to tilt the pelvis forward, relieves tension from the lower back, and helps you to keep a more upright position.

- If kneeling, lift the buttocks and place a cushion between the back of the thighs and the top of the calves. This can make kneeling much more comfortable. If you prefer, you can sit with your back against a wall or use a chair. You want to be comfortable and to be able to keep the spine erect.

Focusing the Mind

- Check your posture. Make sure there is no unnecessary tension in the legs. Have the weight centered. Relax the belly. Lengthen through the spine. Drop the shoulders down and back. Relax the face. A very slight smile allows the face to relax a little more.

- Take a deep breath. Let it out with a sigh and a sense of letting go of all physical and mental tension.

- Bring the awareness to the breath at the tip of the nose. Notice the cool air coming in and the warm air going out. Don't force the breath; simply watch its natural flow. As you sit still, the breath will slow down and the mind will become calm.

- After a minute or so you can gently begin to warm up the body.

- Taking a little time to warm up the body will help to prevent injury and strain and enable you to be more flexible and supple in the postures. Take a few minutes to check out the body to see if there are any sensitive areas that need extra care during your Hatha yoga session.

Netra Vyaayaamam (Eye Movements)

Hatha yoga works all parts of the body—even the eyes. The eye movements help to strengthen and tone the muscles of the eyes and the optic nerves. They help to relieve stressed and tired eyes and, if practiced regularly, can help to improve the eyesight. These are great movements to do throughout the day, particularly if you work with computers. They will refresh the eyes and help to improve concentration.

Before you begin, remove eyeglasses and hard contact lenses. You will be moving the eyes in all directions—taking them to the dark edges of the vision. Only go as far as is comfortable without strain.

Vertical Movements

- Keeping the head still, look up, and then down. Repeat eight times.
- Bring the eyes to center and then close them. Let the eyes rest a moment.

Horizontal Movements

- Keeping the head still and the shoulders relaxed, open the eyes and look to the far right.
- Move the eyes across the center of vision to the left, trying to move them in a straight line. Repeat eight times.
- Bring the eyes back to center and close them.

Full Circular Movements

- Open the eyes and look straight up—as if to 12 o'clock.
- Slowly rotate the eyes clockwise as if looking at all the numbers on the face of a clock. If you find the eyes jumping, this indicates a weakness in the muscles, and you need to move the eyes a little more slowly. Repeat four times.
- Bring the eyes around to the top, then center and close them.
- Open the eyes, look up, and slowly rotate them counterclockwise. Be sure to make complete circles with the eyes.

Resting and Relaxing the Eyes

- Keeping the eyes closed, rub the palms together briskly to make them warm.
- Cup the eyelids with the palms, fingers extended into the hairline. Let the eyes rest in the warmth and darkness.
- When the warmth fades, gently stroke the eyelids a few times with the tips of the fingers in the direction of the ears. Soothe the eyes that work so hard for you all day, every day.

Neck and Shoulder Rolls

Most people tend to hold a lot of physical tension in the neck and shoulders. These gentle movements help to loosen these areas, preparing them for the postures. Gently massage the muscles in the neck and upper back. You can repeat them as often as necessary.

Neck

1

Drop the head forward. Let the weight of the head gently stretch the neck and upper back. Count to five. Lift the head.

2

Drop the right ear toward the right shoulder—don't force or strain. As you exhale tell the neck to let go. Count to five. Lift the head.

3

Drop the left ear toward the left shoulder. Keep the shoulders relaxed. Count to five. Lift the head.

4

Drop the head forward. Gently and slowly roll the head over to the right.

5

Then down and over to the left. Repeat twice each side, or more if necessary.

Shoulders

1

Place the fingertips on the shoulders,
elbows pointing toward the floor.

2

Breathing in, bring the elbows up in front of
you to shoulder level—higher if comfortable.

3

Take the arms back, expanding the chest.
Breathe out as you take the elbows around
and down. Making large circular
movements, repeat four to six times.

Repeat, rotating in the opposite direction.

Back and Arm Stretch

1

Sitting upright, have the hands in the lap
and clasp the fingers together.

2

Take a deep breath in as
you stretch the arms out
in front, pushing the palms
away from you.

3

Lift the arms up over the head, stretch up
and look up. Hold for a count of three to five.

4

Exhaling, unclasp the fingers, and bring the arms down, stretching them out to the sides. Stretch the fingers as well. Drop the head forward.

Repeat two to four times.

Practice these warm-up movements throughout the day to help prevent the physical manifestations of stress. Instead of having a chocolate bar or cake mid-morning, have a stretch break. Get your work colleagues to join in. You will energize the body, clear the head, and improve concentration and clarity of thought. If you prevent tension from building up in your body and mind during the day, you won't feel so exhausted at the end of the day.

There are a couple of other good movements to add to your office routine. Simply pump the feet up and down and then rotate the ankles both clockwise and counterclockwise. This helps to prevent blood pooling in the feet and improves the circulation.

If you type a lot, simply stretch out the arms and fingers, hold for a count of three, and then relax. Repeat four times. It's a good idea to take a stretch break for one minute every hour.

Pelvic Rock (Cat and Cow)

We now want to loosen the back and spine. These pelvic tilting movements help to keep the spine flexible and strong, removing discomfort and tension. They also help to release tension and pressure from the nerves that extend from the spine. If you have been suffering with stress, these simple movements will help facilitate the correct functioning of the parasympathetic nervous system.

1

Come to the hands and knees. Hands should be about shoulder width apart, fingers spread out and pushed evenly into the floor. Do not lock the elbows. Have the knees the same width apart as the hands and part the feet. If you are prone to getting cramps in the feet, keep the toes curled under.

2

Inhale. As you exhale, look down and back toward the knees. At the same time, tilt the pelvis forward, arching the back up.

3

Inhale. Look up toward the ceiling and tilt the pelvis back, gently arching the back.

Imagine a cat stretching out. Breathe deeply and try to harmonize the movement with the breath—this will help to concentrate and calm the mind. Repeat four to six times.

Variations

1

Exhale and turn the upper body to the right. Look back toward the heels as you stretch the hips to the left.

2

Inhale and bring the upper body and hips back to the center. Exhale and turn the upper body to the left and the hips to the right. Repeat four to six times.

1

Exhale and turn the head, upper body, and hips to the right.

2

Inhale, bringing the head and body back to center. Exhale and turn the head, upper body, and hips to the left.

- Keep alternating bringing the head and hips toward each other. Repeat four to six times.

- These variations increase the benefits of the Pelvic Rock by toning the muscles along the sides of the body. They work on the cranial nerves and massage the kidneys and the adrenal glands.

Child's Pose

This is a gentle, nurturing pose to finish off your warm up. It gives a wonderful stretch to the spine and eases discomfort from the back. It is particularly effective for releasing tension in the lower back. The Child's Pose also gives a gentle massage to the abdominal area and can be very comforting during menstruation.

1

Move into the Child's Pose from the Pelvic Rock.

2

Keep the hands on the floor and slowly sit back on the heels. Feel the stretch through the arms and shoulders.

3

Take the arms behind you and let them rest on the floor, palms up. Relax the shoulders. Hold for 30–60 seconds.

To come up, extend the chin forward and slowly lift up. You can use the hands to help if you need to.

Take a deep breath and exhale with a sigh—ahh!

Variation

If you feel too much pressure in the head while holding the Child's Pose, bring the arms forward with the forearms on the floor. Make a couple of fists and stack one on top of the other, then rest the head on top of the fists. If there is too much pressure on the abdominal area, you can try using fists and/or keeping the feet together and parting the knees.

Surya Namaskaram (Sun Worship)

This is a sequence of 12 postures that eventually flow one into one another. The sequence is a great warm up for the body, limbering it up for the following poses and acting as a tonic for the entire system. All the front and back muscles are stretched and toned. The spine is kept flexible and strong, and mobility is improved in the joints. Circulation is improved, and the body and mind are energized.

If you don't have time for a full Hatha yoga session, this is an excellent sequence to do in the morning to wake the body and mind, preparing it for the day. It's also wonderful after a stressful day as it bends and stretches the spine, releasing nervous tension, and helping you to switch off.

It will take a little regular practice to get familiar with the sequence, but stick with it. Once mastered, you can perform the

sequence slowly, really working on stretching each part of the body, or you can speed it up, making it into more of an aerobic activity.

To begin with, you will be fully occupied with trying to figure out how to do the different postures, but eventually you will be able to flow smoothly from one pose to the next in harmony with the breath. I have given instructions for the breath, but don't worry about it until you have mastered the sequence. The general rule for working with the breath is that you breathe in when the chest is expanded or when you are opening out the body and breathe out when you are closing down, folding forward or restricting the chest. Breathe deeply to oxygenate the blood and to produce more energy for the muscles. See chapter 6 for deep three-part breathing, which teaches you how to take in seven times more oxygen than in normal shallow breathing.

Position One

a

Stand with the feet either together or slightly apart and parallel. Weight is evenly distributed between the feet—push the big toes and the outer edges of the heels to the floor. Bring the palms together in front of the chest.

b

Drop the shoulders and stand tall, lengthening through the spine. Feel as if someone is pulling you up by a piece of string at the crown of the head. Stretch both arms out straight in front of you, parallel to the floor.

1a   1b

Position Two

Breathe in. Lock the thumbs and take the arms out and up alongside or close to the ears. Stretch up and bend the knees slightly. Tilt the pelvis forward and bend back a little bit. Don't bend back too far or hold for too long, as you may get dizzy or pass out.

Variation

As you get more advanced, you stretch back farther. Push the pelvis forward as you lean farther back.

Position Three

a

Breathe out. Keeping the back straight and the arms close to the ears with the thumbs still locked, fold forward and down from the hips.

b

Drop the head and hang down. Bring the face in toward the knees.

3a

Variation

As you get more advanced, take hold around the back of the calfs or ankles and pull the torso toward the legs.

Position Four

Breathe in. Bending the knees if you need to, place the palms on the floor on either side of the feet with the fingertips in line with the top of the toes. Don't worry if you can't get the palms on the floor, just place the fingertips down but be sure to keep them in line with the toes. Stretch the left leg as far back as you can and drop the knee to the floor. Sink down through the hips, lunging forward. Keeping the shoulders down, look up and feel as if you are lengthening through the spine.

3b

Position Five

Breathe out. Take the right foot back to meet the left, buttocks raised high so the body forms an angle. Raise up onto the tips of the toes. Take the head between the arms, looking back toward the feet. Slowly push the heels toward the floor.

6a

Position Six

a

Breathe in. Lower the knees to the floor. Keep the toes curled under.

b

Keeping the hips slightly raised, lower the chest and chin. This takes a bit of practice. Women tend to find it difficult as it requires quite a lot of upper body strength—persevere and you will soon get the hang of it.

6b

Position Seven

Hold the breath. By bringing the body weight forward, lower the pelvis down to the floor. Keeping the shoulders down and the elbows bent, lift the head, neck, and chest.

Position Eight

Breathe out. Push back up into the angle position, heels toward the floor and head between the arms.

Position Nine

Breathe in. Swing the left foot forward, placing it between the hands. Lower the right knee to the floor. Shoulders down, look up.

Variation
If you can't swing the foot between the hands.

1

Swing the foot forward as far as you can.

2

Lower the right knee to the floor.

3

Then, take the left hand around the back of the left ankle.

4

Then, bring the left foot up a bit closer toward the hands, encouraging the hips to loosen.

10

Position Ten

Breathe out. Bring the right foot forward to meet the left. Keep the knees bent if you need to and bring the face in toward the knees.

11a

11b

Position Eleven

a

Breathe in. Lock the thumbs. Keeping the arms alongside the ears and with a straight back, stretch out and lift up.

b

Bend the knees, push the pelvis forward, and bend back slightly. This is quite an advanced stretch.

Position Twelve

- Breathe out and return to normal breathing. Bring the palms to rest in front of the chest in prayer position. Lower the arms alongside the body, step to the side, close the eyes, and relax.

- Observe how the body is feeling. Imagine that warm, tingling sensation is white light— prana (the vital life force). Repeat the sequence three times, or more if you want to.

- After Surya Namaskaram, you can lie down in Savasana, Relaxation Pose, or you can do one of the standing postures. How do you feel? If you are quite breathless, it would probably be a good idea to take a rest, otherwise let the breath return to normal and then proceed with one or two standing poses.

12

Savasana (Relaxation Pose)

It is a good idea to rest between poses. This allows the body to relax completely, so you can revitalize the system and not become exhausted. It allows the blood to flow freely, washing away toxins released while holding the postures, and gives you an opportunity to observe the effects of the preceding pose and assimilate the benefits.

- Lie on your back with the legs at least shoulder width apart. This encourages the hips to relax and releases tension from the lower back.

- Have the arms away from the body with the palms turned up, allowing the shoulders to relax and sink toward the floor.

- Find a comfortable place to rest the head. Use a cushion if you prefer.

- Keeping the head on the floor, lower the chin toward the chest to lengthen, and relax the neck.

- Take a deep breath and let it out through the mouth with a sigh—ahh.

- Mentally tell the body to let go.

- Observe the effects of the postures. If you feel any tension or discomfort, breathe into that area, and on the exhalation, tell that part of the body to relax. (See chapter 5, yoga nidra [deep relaxation] for a more detailed explanation.)

Standing Poses

Vrikshasana (Tree Pose)

This is a balancing pose, and like all balancing poses, the main benefits are in improving balance, purifying the nervous system, and concentrating the mind. Balancing forces you to focus the mind— you will discover that if you concentrate, you will balance—if the mind wanders, then so will the body. It is usually more difficult to balance if you have had a stressful day. The Tree Pose tones the legs, strengthening the bones and joints. It also helps to open the hips, expands the chest, loosens the shoulders, and tones the arms.

Supporting Foot Position

Place the weight on the right foot.
Spread the toes and make sure the weight
is evenly distributed.

Raised Foot Positions

1

If you find balancing difficult, place the ball of
the left foot on top of the right foot. Pressing
down makes balancing easier, lightly placing
the foot on top makes it more difficult.

2

Place the left foot on the inside of the right
knee. The raised knee points out to the side.

3

Place the sole of the raised foot on the inside
of the supporting thigh. Push both legs
together. Be careful not to push the supporting
hip out to the side and out of alignment. Work
the raised knee back, opening the hip.

As you progress, you can eventually
place the top of the raised foot on the front
of the supporting thigh where the thigh
meets the hip. The knee points down.

Arm Positions

1

Bring the palms together in front of the chest. Shoulders down and back. Lift and spread the chest.

2

When steady in position 1, keep the hands together and raise the arms over the head with the elbows bent. Work on bringing the elbows back while keeping the palms together and the shoulders down.

Eventually you will be able to keep the hands together over the head and straighten the elbows. Hold steady and breathe deeply.

Coming Out of the Pose

- It is important to come out slowly and smoothly in order to maintain the benefit of a balancing pose. Slowly lower the arms, then the leg.

- You may want to take the weight off the supporting leg and gently wiggle to relieve any tension and to relax the muscles. To begin with, hold the pose for 20–30 seconds. Repeat, standing on the left foot.

Tree Pose Continued . . .

Balance

To help you balance, fix your gaze on a spot on the floor or on the wall in front. Count your breath, letting it become smooth and deep.

If you find it particularly difficult to keep your balance, the pose can be performed with the straight leg alongside a wall. Stand quite close to the wall and perform the pose as above. If you lose your balance, you can rest the raised elbow on the wall to steady yourself. You can also use this technique with the raised knee toward the wall or standing with the heels toward the wall, about 4 inches (10 cm) away. Lean back on the wall and bring the raised foot into position. Bring the palms together in front of the chest and then straighten up pushing away from the wall. When you lose your balance, lean back on the wall again. Some students find that standing near the wall improves the balance—it seems to help just knowing the wall is there.

Natarajasana (King Dancer Pose)

This pose maintains and builds balance and improves concentration. It also strengthens and tones the legs and opens the hips and shoulders.

1

Bring the weight onto the right foot. Spread the toes and evenly distribute the weight.

2

Fix the gaze. Bend the left knee and take hold of the ankle or foot behind you with the left hand. Stand up tall, lifting the chest.

3

Raise the right arm up toward the ceiling, taking it back toward the ear. Stretch through the arm, but be sure to keep the shoulder down.

Once you feel steady, begin to push the left foot into the hand, lifting the foot up and away from the body. Stretch through the torso, expanding and lifting the chest. Lengthen and gently arch the back. If you are steady, look up toward the ceiling.

As with the Tree Pose, you can stand close to a wall and lean against it if the balance is lost. The left foot would be about 6 inches (15 cm) from the wall.

Coming Out of the Pose

Come out slowly in reverse order so as not to dissipate the balanced, focused energy. If you feel the need, you can ease tension from the supporting leg and raised arm, but do this gently—again so you do not disperse the energy. To begin with, hold the pose for 4–10 seconds.

Trikonasana (Triangle Pose)

The Triangle Pose helps to open the hips, chest, and shoulders. It elongates the spine, giving it a wonderful lateral stretch. The muscles of the legs are stretched and toned, and the intercostal muscles of the rib cage are developed. This pose gives a nice squeeze to the digestive system and helps to tone the waist. It can also help relieve backache and menstrual cramps.

1

Part the legs nice and wide, about 4 feet (1.2 m) apart. Turn the right foot out to 90 degrees, and with the left heel on the floor, turn the left foot in a little. Make sure the heel on the right foot lines up with the instep on the left. Place the hands on the hips and make sure the hips and shoulders face the front.

2

Inhale. Take the arms up and over the head, lifting the rib cage.

3

Exhale, bringing the arms down to shoulder level, parallel to the floor. Make sure the shoulders are down. Tighten the thigh so the right quadriceps are lifting the kneecap.

4

Exhale. Push the pelvis to the left while extending the torso to the right as far as you can, bringing the torso over the right leg. Make sure both hips are still facing the front.

5

Take the right hand down to the leg as far as you can comfortably reach. The left arm points up toward the ceiling with the palm turned in to face you.

6

Rotate the top shoulder back. Relax into the pose. With each exhalation, work the rotation. Feel as though you are extending the entire spine from the sacrum out through the crown of the head.
If comfortable, turn your head to look up toward the left palm. If the neck becomes uncomfortable, look toward the floor.

- Make sure you keep the shoulders relaxed and pulled down away from the ears. The bend should come from the hips and not the waist. If trying to keep the hips level causes too much strain on the back hip, let it rotate forward a little. After a few breaths, try to gently rotate it back again.

Coming Out of the Pose

- Inhale. Lift up with the arms out to the sides.

- Relax the arms and take a deep breath.

- Reverse the feet—left foot out, right foot in—and repeat on the left side. To begin with, hold the pose for 4–10 breaths—about 15 seconds—each side.

Variations

If your shoulders become uncomfortable, put your hand back on your hip. Look to the floor if there is discomfort in the neck.
- To protect the knees, turn the back foot in more.

- The lower arm can rest on the thigh or the shin. If you like, you can rest the hand on a block or chair.

- Trikonasana can be practiced against a wall to help keep the torso and legs on the same plane. Place the left heel against the wall and have the right heel opposite the left arch. Work to keep the right hip and shoulder blades against the wall. Don't force the left hip to make contact with the wall. Think about drawing the right hip back toward the left heel.

Virabhadrasana II (Warrior II)

There are three warrior poses. We are only going to practice one as the others are a little more advanced. Virabhadrasana builds strength and stamina. The Warrior Pose strengthens and tones the calf, quadriceps, and buttock muscles. It opens the hips and shoulders, tones the arms, and expands the chest, increasing lung capacity and stretching the muscles of the chest. The abdominal muscles and organs are toned, aiding digestion. The circulation and the flow of energy throughout the body are improved.

1

Part the legs about 4 feet (1.2 m). Keeping the heels on the floor, turn the right foot out to 90 degrees and the left foot in a little. Make sure the right heel is in line with the arch of the left foot.

2

Inhale and take the arms up and over the head, lifting the rib cage.

3

Exhale, bringing the arms down to shoulder level, parallel to the floor palms facing down. Stretch the arms, keeping the shoulders down and back.

4

Exhaling, bend the right knee to form a right angle—or as close as you can get. To protect the knee, make sure it does not extend out over the ankle and does not rotate out of alignment with the foot.

• Keep the back foot pushed to the floor. Including the little toe, extend the leg from the heel to the buttock. Make sure the weight is spread evenly between the feet. Gently draw the left hip back, working the hip joints. Turn the head to look along and beyond the right arm.

With each inhalation, feel as if you are lifting the chest and lengthening the spine, extending up out of the pelvis.

• Exhaling, open the chest and stretch the arms, making sure they stay aligned with each other. Make sure the back arm does not drop toward the floor.

As you breathe deeply, working the pose, you can mentally repeat a positive affirmation, such as, "I am confident, I am strong." Hold the pose steady, breathing evenly and deeply for 4–10 breaths or 15–30 seconds.

Coming Out of the Pose

• Inhale, straightening the right leg.

• Lower the arms and turn to face the center.

• Reverse the position of the feet and repeat on the left side.

Variations

• To begin with, you can perform the pose against a wall. With the left heel against a wall, place the outer edge of the right foot about 2 inches (5 cm) away from the wall and parallel to it. The legs are about 4 feet (1.2 m) apart. Keeping the arms, shoulder blades, and right buttock in contact with the wall, bend the right knee, so it is parallel to the wall and extends out over the right foot.

• You may not be able to take such a wide stance to begin with—just work with what is comfortable for you.

• It might be too much of a strain to have the front knee at a right angle at first. That's quite normal. Bend as far as is comfortable without strain, but do check that the knee doesn't stick out over the ankle. Allow the back hip to come forward a little to avoid strain and to stabilize the front knee over the ankle.

• If you feel any discomfort in either knee, come up out of the pose.

If you have performed one or two standing poses after the Sun Worship, take a minute to rest in Savasana (Relaxation Pose) before continuing with the next section.

Backward Bending Poses

After Savasana, roll over onto your front with the head to one side and the arms alongside the body, palms up. The legs can be any comfortable distance apart. If you are prone to getting cramps in the feet, keep the toes curled under. Relax the shoulders, buttocks, and legs.

This is the relaxation position on the front. If your neck is uncomfortable, bring the arms up, hands one on top of the other, and rest the cheek on the hands or keep the forehead on the floor.

When you rest in between the back bends, alternate the cheek you place on the floor to give both sides of the neck an equal stretch.

Bhujangasana (Cobra Pose)

The Cobra Pose helps to keep the spine flexible and strong, and is particularly good for strengthening the muscles of the upper back. Each vertebra and attached ligament is pulled backward, flushing it with blood, and making minor adjustments to the spine. The pose tones and brings blood to the deep superficial muscles of the back. It releases nervous energy up and down the spinal column and relieves back fatigue. Bhujangasana expands the chest and improves the posture, helping to prevent kyphosis — the rounding of the upper back. The abdominal muscles are stretched and abdominal pressure is increased. This helps to tone the abdominal organs and improves movement through the bowels. The circulation of blood to the sexual and reproductive organs is increased, which helps to prevent disorders of the uterus, ovaries, and testes.

1

Bring the legs together, forehead to the floor. Place the hands underneath the shoulders with the fingers facing forward and in line with the top of the shoulders. The forearms should be off the floor with the elbows pointing in toward the body. Toes are stretched out unless you get cramps in the feet.

2

Work the feet toward the wall behind you to stretch and lengthen the lower back, and extend the chin forward. Lengthening the spine and creating space prevents you from compressing the vertebrae.

3

Inhale and, without using the hands, lift the head and chest. Lengthen the neck. Keep the shoulders down and back. Keep the buttocks relaxed and the heels together. This ensures the hips and muscles in the lower back are aligned.

Hold the pose steady and keep the breath even. With each inhalation, feel as if you are elongating the spine and creating space between each vertebra.

With each exhalation, drop the shoulders, expanding the chest, and gently take the head back as far as is comfortable without compressing the neck.

Concentrate between the shoulder blades at the top of the back. Hold for 4–10 breaths, or 15–20 seconds. Repeat twice.

Coming Out of the Pose

- Extending the chin forward, slowly lower down. Bring the chin to the floor first, then the forehead.

- Place the head to one side, release the arms alongside the body and relax the upper back. As you exhale, mentally tell the upper back to "relax" or to "let go."

Variations

- If the neck feels as if it is being compressed, look toward the floor slightly.

- If the lower back feels uncomfortable, let the heels part. If you still feel compression, try parting the legs.

- Push the pelvis into the floor. Tighten the buttocks.

- If the knees feel uncomfortable, keep the toes curled under.

- If you have kyphosis, or hunched shoulders, look down, bring the arms back and shoulders toward each other.

Ardha Slabasana (Half Locust Pose)

The Half Locust Pose is great for strengthening the muscles of the lower back. If you have weak back muscles, they will not support the spine properly. As you get older, the simplest movement, like stretching up to open a window, can be enough to put the back out of alignment and cause much discomfort. The vertebrae and nerves extending from the spine in the lumbosacral region are nourished with fresh oxygenated blood. Abdominal pressure is very high, increasing the benefits started with the Cobra Pose and helping the stomach, liver, pancreas, kidneys, and uterus to work effectively. This helps to relieve constipation. The elasticity of the lungs is improved as oxygen is forced into idle cells, and a fresh supply of blood is brought to the brain and facial tissues.

Variations

- If you have arthritis of the elbows or wrists, keep the arms alongside the body with the palms down.

- If you are overweight also keep the arms alongside the body.

- Buxom women should place the arms so the breasts are pushed together and up. The arms should be on the outside of the breasts and not pressing into them.

1

Extend the chin out on the floor. Rocking from side side, tuck the arms underneath the body. Try to kee the elbows straight and as close together as possib If possible, lock the thumbs and have the palms against the thighs. You can have the palms down o you can make a couple of fists. However, both of these positions promote the tendency to use the upper body strength to lift the legs. Bring the legs together. This encourages the muscles close to the spine to work.

2

Exhale. Stretch out the right leg and, without pushing down on the left, lift the right leg up.
Keep the knee straight. Bending the knee works the leg but takes the work off the lower back.

Keep the weight balanced between the hips. Do not lift the right hip up high rotating it backward— keep the hips level. Keep the chin on the floor. Concentrate on the lower back. Make sure you are not tensing anything unnecessarily. Concentrating, release the leg and bring the feet together.

- Repeat with the left leg. Hold each leg up for 10 seconds. Alternating, do the pose twice on each side.

Salabasana (Locust Pose)

The Locust Pose deepens and increases the benefits of the Half Locust Pose. You may find this pose particularly difficult to begin with. If that is the case, persevere with the Half Locust Pose until lower back strength develops.

After the Half Locust Pose, keep the hands in position and bend the elbows, taking a brief rest.

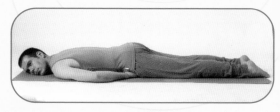

1

Prepare as for Half Locust Pose—chin on the floor, arms tucked under the body and legs together.

2

Exhale, tense, and swing both legs up. Keep the knees straight. Eventually you want to be able to hold a piece of paper between them. Keep the awareness at the lower back. Hold for 10–15 seconds.

Lower the legs, release the arms, and place the head to one side. Relax the lower back.

Poorva Nauasana
(Backward Boat Pose)

This is a good preparatory pose for the Bow
Pose, which comes next.

1

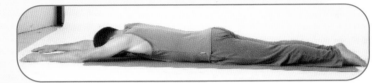

Lie on your front and place the forehead on the
floor, legs together and arms stretched out in
front with the palms on the floor. Stretching out
the body, walk the legs to the wall behind you
and stretch the arms out in front.

2

Inhale and lift up both halves of the body,
balancing on the abdomen. If you need to, let the
legs part but keep the knees straight. Keep the
shoulders down and back. Keep the head up
without compressing the neck. Breathe while
holding the pose, keeping the awareness on the
spine or belly. Hold for 15–20 seconds. Repeat if
you want.

3

Lower down. Take the arms down
alongside the body and place the head
to one side. Remember to alternate the cheek
placed on the floor. Relax the back.

Dhanurasana (Bow Pose)

The Bow Pose combines and deepens the benefits of the Cobra and Locust Poses. Elasticity of the spine is often lost as we get older and because of poor diet and stress. Practicing the backward bends, particularly the Bow Pose, can greatly improve this elasticity. The solar plexus area is revitalized and the massaging and stretching of the abdominal area relieves the sensations of anxiety we sometimes feel in the abdomen. This posture also massages the liver, pancreas, kidneys, and adrenals. Massaging the internal organs is as beneficial and relaxing as having your back massaged. Toxins and tension are released from the organs helping them to work more effectively. The Bow Pose tones the legs, buttocks, and arms. It also strengthens the hips and shoulders.

1

Bring the forehead to the floor and bend the knees, bringing the heels toward the buttocks.

2

Reach back and take hold of the feet, ankles, or legs. You may find you need to part the legs to begin with.

3

With a contraction of the calves and thighs, push the feet into the hands and see if you can lift the legs, head, and chest off the floor. Make sure you lift the legs first. Lifting the head and chest first makes it more difficult to raise the legs.

Working With the Pose

- You need to push the feet up and away from the body, straightening the elbows. It is common to pull the feet in toward the buttocks. This makes it practically impossible to lift the legs off the floor.

- Allow the shoulders to be drawn down and back.

- Apart from the legs, the rest of the body should remain relaxed. Do not use any undue effort. The arms are just linking the ankles to the shoulders.

- Feel the weight of the body settle into the center of the belly.

- To lift the legs higher, try keeping them hip-distance apart to begin with, lifting the chest and feet up toward the ceiling.

- With practice you will be able to bring the feet, then the knees, and eventually the legs together.

- Once you can take hold of the feet easily try working the hands down toward the ankles and then down onto the legs. This helps to bring the knees up higher and level with the shoulders, which in turn helps to bring the weight onto the abdomen, enhancing the benefits, instead of keeping the weight on the pelvic area.

- Breathe gently. Eventually the body will gently rock backward as you breathe in and forward as you breathe out. This increases the massage effect on the abdominal area.

- Keep the awareness either on the length of the spine or on the abdomen. Hold for 15–20 seconds. Repeat if you like.

- Coming down, release the legs and place the arms alongside the body with the head to one side.

- Relax the back.

Variations

To begin with, you may find it is enough just to hold the preparatory position, without lifting the legs up off the floor.

- If you cannot reach the feet, try taking hold of the bottom edge of your pants or socks.

- Another alternative is to lean on one forearm and reach back with the other, arching one side of the body at a time and keeping the knees apart. (shown on right, steps 1, 2, and 3).

- If you can reach the feet but the legs won't come off the floor, try moving the hands down the legs. This may help to lift them up.

Some teachers recommend using a belt wrapped around the ankles or feet to help lift up into the pose. You can try this if you like, but you should be aware that you tend to use the strength of the arms to lift up. Using a belt also pulls the feet in toward the buttocks instead of lifting them up and away. This creates a different stretch and can put undue strain on the knees. If you find the Bow Pose strenuous, you could practice the Backward Boat Pose.

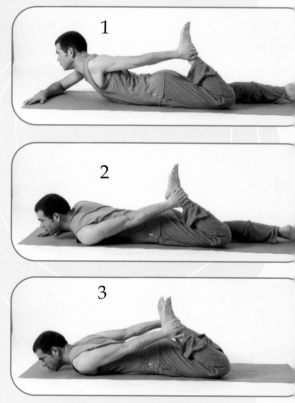

Relax After the Backward Bends

- After the backward bending postures, roll over onto the back and lie in Savasana (Relaxation Pose) for one minute. Observe the effects of the backward bends and allow the body to relax. Mentally scan the body from the toes to the head, checking for any tension or discomfort. Breathe into those areas. On the exhalation, tell that part of the body to let go.

Sitting Up Safely

- To sit up for the forward bends, bring the legs together. Then, you can slip the hands under the small of the back, palms on the floor. Lift the head and chest. Pushing down evenly on the palms, help yourself to sit up, (shown to the right).

- Alternatively, if your back and stomach muscles are strong, take the arms overhead and lock the thumbs. Breathing in, stretch, keeping the arms close to the ears and the legs to the floor. Hold the breath and sit up. The arms may come down in front of you to begin with, but as the stomach muscles strengthen, you will be able to keep the arms by the ears.

   If your back is quite sensitive, it is safer to roll to one side and help yourself up by using the hands.

Forward Bending Poses
Janusirshasana (Head to Knee Pose)

The Head to Knee Pose gives a wonderful stretch to the entire back of the body from the head to the feet. It's a great pose for relieving pressure from the lower back caused by sitting for extended periods of time. Pressure is released and circulation improved to the parasympathetic nerves, which extend from the lower back, improving the relaxation response. The hamstring muscles at the back of the leg are stretched. Janusirshasana aids digestion and helps to relieve constipation. Circulation to all the abdominal organs is improved and the thoracic, spine, and the intercostal muscles of the ribs are stretched.

1

Make sure you are sitting on the "sitting" bones with both legs stretched out in front.

2

Keeping the right leg straight, bend the left knee and bring it up toward the chest. Hugging the leg, lengthen through the spine, shoulders down.

3

Let go of the left leg and let the knee drop down toward the floor, keeping the hips level. Place the sole of the left foot along the inside of the right thigh. Keep the knee and toes on the right leg pointing up toward the ceiling. Push the back of the knee toward the floor.

4

Take the arms out to the sides and up overhead, locking the thumbs. If the shoulders are a little tight, keep the hands shoulder-distance apart. Inhaling, stretch up and look up, lifting the rib cage.

5

Exhaling, maintain the extension through the spine as you fold forward from the hips over the right leg. Be aware of the pelvis rotating over the hip joints.

6

Take hold of the leg, ankle, or foot—wherever you can comfortably reach without straining.

If you can't reach the foot, keep the elbows straight to encourage the torso to move forward. Once you can take hold of the foot, relax the elbows toward the floor. You are aiming to have the sternum in the middle of the chest, centered over the right leg. Relax the shoulders and the neck.

- If you feel strain in the back of the leg, bend the knee a little and gently work with the breath, gradually stretching out the leg.
- If there is discomfort in the lower back, come up a little. Working with the breath, slowly relax forward and down.
- Let the breath be relaxed. With each inhalation, let the torso lift slightly. As you exhale, feel as if the spine is extending forward and down as you bring the abdomen closer to the thigh, relaxing into the pose.

Coming Out of the Pose

- To come out, lock the thumbs and bring the arms up toward the ears. Inhale, stretch forward a little more and, keeping the back straight, lift up.

- Stretch up and then lower the arms down to the sides. Keep sitting nice and tall— don't be tempted to slouch.

- Bring the left knee back up toward the chest and then straighten out the leg.

- Repeat on the right side. Hold each side for 30–45 seconds, or 10–20 breaths.

Variations

If you are very stiff, you may find it useful to sit on the edge of a cushion or a rolled blanket to rotate the pelvis forward. To test for stiffness, check whether your lower back rounds when you sit with both legs extended forward. If it does, sit on something.

It also helps to bend the knee slightly to enable you to bring the torso more over the extended leg.

- When you have finished Janusirshasana, take the arms overhead, lock the thumbs, stretch up, and look up. Lower the chin toward the chest and slowly lower the back to the floor. Try to keep the arms close to the ears and the legs on the floor. If you prefer, you can use the hands to help lower yourself down more gently.

- Rest for 20 seconds with the arms over the head to loosen the shoulders. Sit up again for the full forward bend. As before, either roll to one side, and slip the hands under the back, or keeping the arms over the head, sit up.

Paschimotanasa (Full Forward Bend)

1

Sitting with the legs extended out in front, make sure the "sitting" bones are on the floor. If you find the lower back is rounded, sit on the edge of a cushion or folded blanket.

2

Inhaling, take the arms out to the sides and up over the head. Locking the thumbs, stretch up and look up. Extending up through the spine, lift the rib cage and abdomen.

3

Exhaling and maintaining the extension, fold forward from the hips, leading with the chest and keeping the back straight.

4

Take hold of the legs, ankles, or feet—wherever you can comfortably reach without strain.

Working With the Pose

- If you can't reach the feet, keep the elbows straight. Once you can reach the feet, relax the elbows toward the floor. If you can reach the feet, link the index fingers around the big toes, joining them onto the thumbs, and bend the elbows down toward the floor. This is Chin Mudra, an energy seal (see page 136). Keep the shoulders relaxed and look toward the legs with the eyes closed, bringing the awareness within.

- Think about bringing the torso forward while keeping the knees and back straight. Don't try to get the head onto the knees, as the back will curve.

- Have the awareness on the length of the spine. With each inhalation, breathe from the top of the spine to the base, and with each exhalation, breathe from the base to the top, extending out through the crown of the head. You can imagine a white light moving up and down the spine.

- Think about creating space between each vertebra.

- After you have relaxed into the pose for several breaths, take a deep inhalation so the torso lifts and you can expand the chest. Arch the back a little and look up. Exhale, bending the elbows outward and bring the torso closer to the legs, moving the hips toward the thighs.

- Continue to relax into the pose, working with the breath and keeping the awareness on the length of the spine. Don't pull on the legs and force yourself farther forward. If you strain, the muscles will tighten and you won't be able to stretch so far; if you let the muscles relax, the muscles will stretch naturally. Hold for one minute.

Coming Out of the Pose

To come out, lock the thumbs, bringing the arms toward the ears. Stretch forward a little. Inhale and, keeping a straight back, lift up.

Stretch up and look up. Lower the chin toward the chest and roll down to the floor, keeping the legs down and the arms close to the ears, if possible. Use the hands to help you down if you prefer.

Lower the arms down alongside the body, turning up the palms, part the legs, take a deep breath, and let go.

Variations

Sit on the edge of a rolled blanket or cushion to help rotate the pelvis forward.

Try working the stretch to the back by bending the knees. You can work the back by bringing the torso forward and down over the thighs for several breaths. Then lifting the torso, straighten the knees, and for several breaths work on the stretch through the back of the legs.

The Full Forward Bend gives an extensive stretch to the back of the body from the toes to the head. The stomach, liver, spleen, kidneys, pancreas, bladder, colon, and intestines are squeezed and massaged, toning the organs and flushing away toxins. Digestion and elimination is improved. This is a very relaxing, calming, and nurturing pose. High blood pressure can be reduced and feelings of anxiety are relieved as the solar plexus is massaged. The pose aids the flow of prana through the sushumna (see chapter 6). Paschimotanasana stimulates the nervous system and releases pressure from the network of nerves, extending from the spinal column as the lumbar vertebrae gently separate one from the other.

Paschima Nauasana (Forward Boat Pose)

The Forward Boat Pose is good for strengthening the legs, abdominal, and back muscles, and promoting balance and stamina.

1

Sit on the floor with the knees bent. Place the hands on the backs of the thighs near to the knees. Fix the gaze on the wall in front.

2

Keeping the back straight, lean backward, bringing the feet off the floor, and find your point of balance.

3

Once steady, straighten the knees and let go of the legs. Keep the elbows straight and the hands on either side of the knees. As you become used to the pose, try to straighten the spine all the way through the neck. Lift the chest, bringing the lower back forward.

Variation

When you are steady and comfortable with this posture and the abdominal and back muscles have strengthened through your Hatha yoga practice, you can begin this pose from lying on the floor.

1

Lie with the arms alongside the body, palms flat.

2

Inhale and lift both halves of the body, balancing on the buttocks. Feel as if the breath is lifting you up. Have the arms alongside the knees.

- Make sure you lift the legs to the same degree as the torso. It is common to lift the legs up high and the torso just a little off the floor. If this happens, lower the legs and find a more balanced position.

- Come out of the pose in a balanced and controlled way. The legs and torso should touch the floor at the same time—tricky! Repeat several times, holding for about five seconds, or hold once for 15–30 seconds.

1

- After the forward bending poses, rest in Savasana (Relaxation Pose) for one minute before continuing with the next section.

Inverted Poses
Setu Bandhasana (Bridge Pose)

Strictly speaking, the Bridge Pose is more of a backward bend and can be a great counterpose to the Forward Boat Pose. To begin with, it can be used to loosen the lower back and pelvis. As you progress, the Bridge Pose will give a dynamic stretch to the entire back; it can be used as an alternative to Dhanurasana (Bow Pose). I have decided to include the Bridge Pose in this section because it gives the body a partial inversion and serves as a wonderful preparation for shoulder stand for students who are a little stiff in the neck and shoulder area. My father, who is in his 70s, finds that if he does the Bridge Pose first, he is then able to swing up into the shoulder stand.

Setu Bandhasana spreads the chest and opens the shoulders, pulling them back, and loosens the upper back. It is also a great pose for toning the legs and buttocks, particularly if you hold the pose in the raised position and give the buttocks a squeeze. As you progress in the pose, lifting more onto the shoulders and neck, the thyroid gland at the base of the throat will be massaged and regulated.

It is probably best not to do this pose if you have your period. Inverting the abdominal area during menstruation, in some cases, can cause flooding and you are also encouraging the body to go against the flow of nature, which is not what yoga is about.

Stage 1

1

Lying on the back, keep the head on the floor and bring the chin down toward the chest to lengthen the neck. Bend the knees and place the soles of the feet on the floor. The feet should be about hip-width apart, parallel, and pointing forward. If you have a sensitive back, keep the feet away from the buttocks. If the back is fine and to work the spine more, bring the feet close toward the buttocks, but make sure the knees point over the feet and do not drop out to the sides. The hips, knees, and ankles should align. Have the arms alongside the body with the palms flat. Stretch the arms down, taking the shoulders away from the ears.

2

Press the lower back into the floor. Notice how the pelvis tips back, how the hips rock, and how the tailbone rolls up. Then arch the lower back, tilting the pelvis and hips forward and moving the tailbone toward the floor. This movement is sometimes called the Pelvic Rock. If you are very stiff in the lower back and hips, repeat the movement 5–10 times. It is also a good movement to include in your warm up.

Stage 2

1

Preparing as for stage 1, push the lower back into the floor and then continue to roll the back off the floor as if you are lifting one vertebra at a time.

2

Lift the hips up toward the ceiling as high as is comfortable. If you feel any discomfort in the back, come down a little. Make sure you keep the hips, knees, and ankles aligned.

- To warm up the body, perform this movement very slowly and dynamically, i.e. slowly, rolling up and down four times. Try to breathe in as you roll up and out as you roll down. Each time, come a little higher and harmonize the movement with the breath. Concentrate on the entire length of the spine.

- After the fourth lift, hold for 10–15 seconds and then slowly roll down again vertebra by vertebra.

Stage 3

Stage 1 works the lower back, stage 2 brings the stretch up to the middle back and shoulder blade area, and stage 3 brings the arch to the upper back and shoulders and stretches the neck, bringing the chin more toward the chest and massaging the thyroid gland.

1

Come up as in stage 2 and hold the pose. Bring the arms underneath the body and clasp the fingers together. Carefully straighten the elbows, pulling the shoulders down and back and spreading the chest. This helps you to increase the arch to the back and brings the weight more onto the shoulders. Push the hips up toward the ceiling. If your back feels uncomfortable, walk the feet away from the shoulders. If the back feels fine, walk the feet closer toward the shoulders and push the hips up further. Keep the feet flat on the floor. Keep the hips, knees, and ankles aligned.

2

When the hips are lifted high enough, you can unclasp the fingers. Bend the elbows, place the hands on the lower back for support, and increase the arch to the back. If the knees start to spread, you have come up too high. Adjust your position and hold steady. Hold for 15–30 seconds.

Coming Out of the Pose

To come out of the pose, return the hands alongside the body, palms flat. If you have brought the feet in toward the shoulders, move them away a little. Slowly roll the back down vertebra by vertebra.

Variations

Placing a folded blanket under the shoulder area may make the pose more comfortable. If using a folded blanket, make sure the neck and head are over the edge of the padding (the top of the blanket should be in line with the top of the shoulders). As well as making things more comfortable for the shoulder blade area, it is particularly effective if you have a stiff neck.

● You may feel the need to counterpose to ease any tension from the back. If this is the case, you can perform the Wind-Eliminating Pose (see page 118).

Pavanamuktasana (Wind-eliminating Pose)

1

Lie down with legs together, arms alongside the body, and palms flat.

2

Bring both knees up toward the chest and wrap the arms around the legs.

3

Exhaling, lift the head toward the knees and bring the knees toward the chest.

4

Inhaling, lower the head to the floor and release the pull on the legs, keeping the arms around the legs.

● When you have completed the Bridge and Wind-eliminating Poses, relax in Savanasana and take a deep breath.

Variations

Some people like to inhale, hold the breath, and then lift up. Exhale as the hold is released. This is particularly effective for relieving wind but can cause quite a lot of pressure in the body and head, so to be safe, exhale as you lift up and inhale as you lower down. Repeat four times.

Sarvangasana (Shoulder Stand)

This is one of the most effective postures for bringing health and vitality to the body and calmness to the mind. Sarvang means "all parts," and this posture does indeed benefit all parts of the body in some way.

The shoulder stand keeps the spine elasticated and strong, helping to prevent the hardening of the upper spine. It relieves stiffness and tension in the neck and shoulders, and strengthens the muscles in the lower back. Coming out of the pose slowly strengthens the abdominal muscles.

The pituitary gland, located in the head, governs the thyroid gland. Pressure on the thyroid gland helps it to release thyroxin, which regulates the functioning of the reproductive system, circulation, digestion, and respiration. A healthy thyroid is also essential for the regulation of the body's metabolism—the rate at which we burn oxygen and food to produce energy.

Sarvangasana rests and drains the legs and helps to prevent varicose veins and hemorrhoids. It assists lymphatic drainage, helps to keep the correct placement of the abdominal organs, and improves the peristaltic action of the bowels. The Shoulder Stand nourishes the spinal column and the nerves rooted in and extending from the spine with oxygenated blood.

Do not perform the shoulder stand if you have: high blood pressure, glaucoma, recent surgery, neck and back injuries, or if you are menstruating. Leave out this pose if you have a headache or any problems in the head area. If you have any problems with the teeth, mouth, nose, ears, etc. the increased pressure in the head may aggravate the situation.

Variations

a

Instead of the Shoulder Stand you can practice the Bridge Pose (see page 114)— except during menstruation.

b

- Lie on your back and tuck your hands under the hips, palms on the floor. Tilt the pelvis up, flatten the back, and lift your legs up in the air, feet toward the ceiling.

c

- Instead of using the hands, you can place a cushion or two under the hips. If menstruating, use only one cushion.

d

- Place the feet up on a chair.

e

● Start sitting up and lean back on the forearms. Lift the legs, letting the feet rest against a wall.

● Use the arms and legs to swivel round until the legs and buttocks are facing the wall.

● Lie down with the arms away from the body, palms up and the legs a comfortable distance apart. Hold alternatives B, C, and D for three minutes.

Shoulder Stand

1

Lying on the back, keep the head on the floor and bring the chin toward the chest. Place the arms alongside the body, with the palms flat and elbows straight. You can tuck the hands a little under the buttocks. Pull the shoulders down away from the ears.

2

Pushing down on the palms, swing the legs up and over so the buttocks come up off the floor.

Quickly bring the hands to the back for support to prevent you from rolling back down to the floor.

Keeping the legs parallel to the floor, bring the elbows as close together as you can, drawing the shoulders further away from the ears.

3

When you feel steady, lift the legs up into the Shoulder Stand.

To begin with, you may feel a lot of weight on the arms and the legs may not come straight up.

Try not to have the hands hooked around the sides of the body. Instead have the palms on either side of the spine and facing toward the shoulders. The closer you can bring the hands toward the shoulders the more you will be able to straighten up the midsection of the body. Also, check that the elbows do not spread too far out to the sides, as this will make it difficult to straighten the body.

As you get used to the pose and the shoulders loosen, the weight will come more onto the shoulders and less onto the elbows. You will be able to move the hands closer toward the shoulders and take the legs back away from the head, gradually straightening up more.

Once in the Shoulder Stand, keep the legs relaxed so you don't restrict the flow of blood, but keep the knees straight to strengthen the abdomen and lower back. If there is weakness or discomfort in the lower back, then bend the knees a little. Feet should be relaxed.

Coming Out of the Pose

- Lower the legs down over the head, parallel to the floor.

- Lower the arms down, palms flat.

- Using the arms and hands as brakes, slowly roll down the spine vertebra by vertebra.

- When the back is flat, stop and push the small of the back toward the floor. Straighten the knees and try to lower the legs as slowly as possible, or bend the knees and come out more gently (see modifications, page 126).

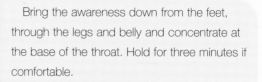

Bring the awareness down from the feet, through the legs and belly and concentrate at the base of the throat. Hold for three minutes if comfortable.

Variations: Coming Into and Holding the Pose

a

1 With the legs up against a wall, bend the knees and place the soles of the feet on the wall.

2 Push on the feet and slowly lift the back off the floor.

3 Bend the elbows and bring the hands to the back. When you feel confident, push the feet away from the wall.

b

If you have a stiff neck, have had neck problems, or simply to make this posture more comfortable, practice on one or more folded blankets, with the neck and head positioned off the end of the blanket.

C

● If you begin to feel discomfort in the lower back while holding the pose, try bending the knees and bringing them toward the forehead.

● Keeping the left leg pointing toward the ceiling, slowly lower the right leg toward the floor. Lift it back up while trying to keep the left leg in position. Repeat with the left leg.

● While holding, slowly part the legs to the sides as if doing the splits. Don't bend at the hips. This is great for stretching the inner thigh.

These leg variations are fun to try, but you will benefit more from holding the posture steady. To begin with, they may enable you to hold the pose for longer, but be aware that you want to develop steadiness.

Modifications:
Coming Out of the Pose

As you lower from the pose, tip the head so the chin points toward the ceiling. This helps to protect the neck.

If you suffer from discomfort in the lower back, roll out of the Shoulder Stand, lower the back to the floor, and stop. Press the small of the back into the floor, bend the knees, and lower the feet close to the buttocks. Then, straighten out the legs.

As you become more flexible, you might like to lower the toes to the floor above the head, straighten the knees and hold. Bring the arms together, clasp the fingers, and gently straighten out the elbows, working the shoulders away from the ears. This is Halasana (Plough Pose). Hold for one minute, then unclasp the fingers, part the arms, and roll down as above. Some students like to perform the Plough Pose before the Shoulder Stand as it helps to bring the weight more onto the shoulders, thus enabling you to straighten the body more in the Shoulder Stand.

Matsyasna (Fish Pose)

The Fish Pose provides an excellent counterpose to the Shoulder Stand, as it stretches the neck and throat in the opposite direction. The muscles in the neck and shoulders are massaged and tension is released. In the Shoulder Stand, the thyroid is compressed, encouraging it to release the hormone thyroxin; in the Fish Pose, it is stretched and the blood carries thyroxin throughout the body. The pituitary and pineal glands, located in the head, are toned and nourished, as are the upper spinal nerves. The chest is expanded and posture improved. It is great for helping to prevent and relieve hunched, rounded shoulders, or kyphosis. Breathing deeply in this posture gets oxygen into the apex of the lungs, helps to get rid of stale, residual air, and builds strength and elasticity in the lungs. This is a good pose to practice if you are asthmatic. Coming in and out of the pose strengthens and tones the neck and throat.

1

Lying on the back, with the elbows straight, grab hold of the outside of the thighs. The fingers slip underneath and the thumbs go up the sides.

2

Push down on the elbows and lift the head and chest off the floor so you are looking down toward the feet. Do not move the elbows, as this position is correct for your body.

Continue to push on the elbows, tilting the pelvis and rolling the hipbones forward. This will arch the lower back.

Push the belly and chest up, arching the back further. Do not move the elbows.

3

Take the head back and lower the crown of the head to the floor. The weight is evenly distributed between the buttocks, elbows, and head. Make sure you do not hunch the shoulders. Keep the legs straight. Don't let them flop outward.

- Breathe deeply into the apex of the lungs. Hold for 30–40 seconds, or 10–20 breaths. Build up until you can hold the pose for one minute.

Coming Out of the Pose

- Bring the weight back onto the elbows. Lift the head off the floor and look toward the feet.

- Slowly lower the back down from the base to the top.

Variations

If you have neck problems or have difficulty getting the head back and to the floor, you can perform the Fish Pose by lying over a blanket roll or several stacked pillows.

1

Sitting up, place the pillows behind you.

2

Grabbing hold of the sides of the pillows or cushions, carefully lower yourself back. You can lean back onto one forearm first and then lower back onto the other.

3

Relax the head back.

4

The neck should be positioned off the end of the pillows. Legs flat.

- If you have asthma you can practice the Fish Pose three times a day building up to five minutes each time. Support the arch in the back with pillows as above. Breathe deeply.

- Counterpose with Pavanamuktasana (Wind-relieving Pose)

- Bend the knees. Hug the legs and bring the head toward the knees and the knees toward the chest. Inhale as you lift up and exhale as you lower down. Repeat four times.

OR

Ardha Pavanamuktasana (Half Wind-relieving Pose)

1

Keeping the left leg straight, bring the right knee up to the chest.

2

Hug the leg and lift the head toward the knee. Pull the knee toward the chest and hold. Keep the shoulders down. Breathe while you hold for 30 seconds. Release and repeat on the other side.

Relax in Savasana (Relaxation Pose) for one minute before continuing with the rotating postures.

Rotating Poses

Ardha Matsyendrasana (Half Spinal Twist)

The Half Spinal Twist strengthens the entire length of the spine and tones all the muscles of the back. The tendons in the neck are twisted, releasing tension, and the muscles of the buttocks are stretched. The nerves of the parasympathetic nervous system and the nerves rooted in the spine are nourished and flushed with freshly oxygenated blood. The joints of the body are strengthened and calcium deposits are prevented from forming on the hips and shoulders. It's a good pose to practice if you suffer with stiff and painful hips. All the vital organs in the body are massaged and toned and toxins are squeezed and flushed out of the intestines. The Half Spinal Twist tones the midriff area and helps to relieve constipation.

1

Sitting on the floor, keep the left leg straight. Bend the right knee, bringing it up toward the chest.

2

Cross the right foot over the left knee. Place the sole of the foot on the floor as close to the outer edge of the left knee as possible. Hugging the right leg, lengthen the spine and drop the shoulders down and back. Bring the chest close to the thigh.

3

Lock the thumbs and stretch the arms out in front.

4

Twist around to the right. Then, place the right hand on the floor behind you with the fingers pointing away. The arm should be close to the body, helping to keep the spine erect. But, at the same time, you need to keep the shoulder down. The position of the right hand will vary from person to person depending on the length of the arms and the flexibility of the spine. Find the position that is comfortable for you.

5

Place the left arm between the torso and the upraised knee. Pushing the left knee to one side, see if you can take hold of the straight leg. Keep the knee and toes on the straight leg pointing up. Lengthen up again and slowly rotate around to the right looking over the right shoulder. Have the awareness on the rotation to the spine.

Hold steady and allow the body to settle into the twist. Breathe in, extending up through the spine. As you exhale, see if you can relax a little farther into the twist. Shoulders are down and well spread.

Coming Out of the Pose

- Look to the front.

- Release the back arm, turning the torso to face the front.

- Release the front arm.

- Take a gentle countertwist to the left.

- Release the raised knee.

- Repeat on the other side. Hold for 30 seconds each side.

Variations

- If you find it difficult to sit up straight, sit on the edge of a cushion or blanket roll.

- To begin with, you may need to take the raised foot toward the ankle and not have it so close to the knee.

- Take the back arm further away from the body or away from the center of the body.

- If you can't take hold of the extended leg, you can hold onto the pants.

OR

- Push the elbow against the upraised knee, with the forearm and hand pointing toward the ceiling or resting along the thigh. Keep the shoulders down.

- As you rotate around push the front arm against the raised knee.

Jathara Parivartanasana (Abdominal Twist)

As well as being a posture in its own right, Jathara Parivartanasana can be used to warm up the body. It's an excellent pose for relieving tension in the spine and the muscles of the back, thus helping to relieve backache. It opens the hips and helps to relax the shoulders. The Abdominal Twist gives a wonderful massage to the abdominal organs, improving digestion and assimilation. It is also a good posture to alleviate constipation.

1

Lie on the back with legs together. Extend the arms out to the sides at shoulder level, with the palms flat on the floor.

2

Bend the knees and bring them up toward the chest. Lift the head a little and turn it to the left. Lower the head, relaxing the neck. Let the ear move gently toward the floor.

3

Exhale, keeping the knees bent, and lower both legs to the floor. Don't hold the feet up, but let them rest on the floor. This may mean that you have to take the knees away from the chest a little. Relax the legs, the back, and the shoulders. If comfortable, keep the left shoulder on the floor; otherwise let it lift as it needs to. Keep checking to make sure you are not holding any unnecessary tension in the body, particularly the shoulders. Tell the body to "let go."

Coming Out of the Pose

- Bring the head and knees back to center.

- Repeat on the other side. Hold for about 10 breaths each side, or 30–40 seconds.

- Straighten out the legs.

- Take a deep breath. If you feel the need, you can bend the knees and hug the legs.

Variations

- If you have a sensitive back, bend the knees and, instead of bringing them up toward the chest, place the soles of the feet on the floor. Take the knees down to the floor, as above, and use the right hand to gently pull the thighs down.

- If you feel comfortable with the stretch, alternating, perform twice each side. On the second round, take the knees down and then straighten them, bringing the feet up toward the hand. That's the feet to the hand and not the hand to the feet. If you can comfortably reach the feet, take hold of the big toes. Bend the knees before coming back to center.

Yoga Mudya (Yogic Seal)

Always end your Hatha yoga session with Yoga Mudra. A mudra is a seal; Yoga Mudra seals in the energy instead of allowing it to dissipate. A mudra focuses the energy and concentration at the point over which the mudra is applied. Yoga Mudra helps to release toxins and relieve disorders in the abdominal area. It opens the hips, gives a wonderful stretch to the spine, relieves tension from the lower back and neck, and helps to balance the nervous system. Yoga Mudra, perhaps more importantly, focuses the awareness inward, calming the mind, and helping you to experience a sense of inner peace. It's a wonderful preparation for Yoga Nidra (Deep Relaxation).

1

Sit in a comfortable cross-legged position— either Sukhasana (Comfortable Pose) or Ardha Padmasana (Half Lotus Pose) (see pages 65 and 66). Sit on your cushion if you prefer. Take both hands behind the back and take hold of the right wrist with the left hand. Try to join the left thumb with one of the fingers. Inhaling, lengthen up through the spine, lifting and expanding the chest. Lift the chin slightly.

2

Exhaling, fold forward and down from the hips, leading with the chest. Drop the head and allow the arms to rest on the back. Drop the shoulders. Close the eyes and have the awareness within for one minute.

There are two other mudras you might like to use at this stage.

Chin Mudra
(Symbol of Wisdom)

This is a lovely position for the hands when you are sitting cross-legged. With the hands resting on corresponding knees, palms turned up, bring the thumb and index finger together with the other three fingers pointing downward. This mudra uplifts us bringing us to knowledge.

In Chin Mudra each finger represents an aspect of the individual and life:

Thumb	Higher, true, or universal self.
Index finger	Individual, lower self
Middle finger	Ego
Ring finger	Illusion of the mind
Little finger	Worldly actions and reactions

Chin Mudra is symbolic of the effort made by the lower self (index finger) on the spiritual path; it renounces all worldliness and rises up toward the higher self. Because of the efforts made by the lower self, the higher self (thumb) bends down to meet it.

Vishnu Mudra

This is used in the breathing technique Nadi Suddhi (see page 189). It helps to keep the energy in instead of having it dissipate through the fingers. Make a gentle fist and from the fist release the thumb and the last two fingers.

After your Hatha yoga session all the muscles, ligaments, and tendons have been stretched and toned, all the organs and glands revitalized and nourished, a lot of tension and toxins have been worked out of the body, and the mind has begun to calm down.

To deepen and continue these benefits it is a good idea to add Yoga Nidra (Deep Relaxation), pranayama (breathing techniques), and dhyana (meditation). (See pages 138, 160, and 194.)

chin mudra

vishnu mudra

5

Yoga Nidra
(Deep Relaxation)

Yoga Nidra (Deep Relaxation)

Yoga Nidra is a vital part of Hatha yoga. It is one of, if not the, best stress-reduction techniques there is and it allows the benefits of the Hatha yoga session to be assimilated.

In Yoga Nidra, you are completely relaxing and revitalizing the entire system, allowing the body to heal and access energy. It also helps us to manage stress, relieve pain, and attain peace of mind. Savanasna (Relaxation Pose) is the most relaxed position the body can be in. In this position and during Yoga Nidra the heart, nervous system, and cardiovascular system rest and the blood pressure lowers more than in any other physical position. A relaxed and calm body leads to a relaxed and calm mind. Instead of many thoughts rushing through the mind, they pass slowly, giving you the opportunity to observe them and to make calm, rational decisions and choices, rather than reacting emotionally, erratically, and sometimes irrationally.

We all have different ways in which we relax and indeed what is relaxing for you might not be relaxing for someone else.

One thing is for sure, the more deeply and completely you relax, the more beneficial and longer-lasting the effects.

In our day-to-day lives, how many of us truly relax? Sometimes we might luxuriate in a hot bubble bath; this can be great for relieving physical tension but not so good if you are busy thinking about your day. We might go to the movies or watch television. But watching a horror movie or murder mystery is hardly relaxing! The body reacts to the frights and thrills, more or less, as it would in real life. We might read the newspapers, but I'm sure you would agree there's nothing relaxing about that. We might go to the gym or for a run, but these activities do not truly relax the body and mind; if anything they stress the various systems of the body. Even when you are sitting listening to music the body remains ready to get up and spring into activity. Deep relaxation literally switches everything off; it's like taking a break to "get away from it all." It has been said that 20 minutes of deep relaxation is equivalent to three hours of deep sleep.

Remember that the goal of yoga is to control the mind so we can experience our true self—peace. In order to do this, we have to be able to keep the body still, free from tension and unease. The asanas help us to achieve a healthy, calm, and steady body, preparing us to develop a more inward focus. Yoga Nidra helps us to move from the material world, with all its distractions, that prevents us from realizing our true nature.

In our day-to-day lives, we are familiar with our physical body, but according to yogic philosophy, we have five bodies. In Sanskrit they are called koshas (sheaths). The koshas cover our true blissful real self.

With practice, during Yoga Nidra, you will have a sense of being drawn inward. You will find out for yourself that there is more to you than a physical body—and eventually you will experience inner peace.

To call the koshas "bodies" is a little misleading, although it is a term that is often used for them. They are different levels of energy, or energy vibrating at different frequencies, that serve different functions in life. For most of us, the different levels are not in harmony with each other. Hatha yoga, Yoga Nidra, pranayama, and meditation all help to bring them into balance.

Even pastimes we do to unwind are not necessarily truly relaxing.

The Koshas

The yogis called these sheaths maya kosha. Maya means "illusion." The koshas make up the "veil of illusion" that covers our pure consciousness; it can be discovered and experienced when we peel away the various veils, or coverings. The process has been likened to peeling away the thin layers of an onion to reveal our inner light; that divine spark, or spirit, that resides within all beings.

The five koshas make up the physical, causal, and astral bodies. The physical body is made up of anna maya kosha and prana maya kosha; the astral body is made up of mano maya kosha and vijnana maya kosha; and the causal body is made up of the ananda maya kosha. When you transcend, or breakthrough, the ananda maya kosha you attain samadhi, the super-conscious state, and everything else is left behind.

Anna Maya Kosha

Anna means food, maya means illusion and kosha means sheath. This is the most dense, or gross, kosha and is known as the Food Sheath. We are all aware of the physical body all day and every day, particularly if we have indigestion, an aching back, etc. The physical body is made up of the food we eat. After death the body will decompose and become food again. When we identify with this temporary body we are the farthest away from our true self.

Prana Maya Kosha

Prana is the vital energy, or life force, also known as chi or qi. This vital body is essential to life and gives us vitality. Pranic, or subtle, energy surrounds, goes through, and is within the physical body; it is our aura and enables us to move. When we lift an arm, it is the arm that follows the pranic body. We have the thought (a more subtle form of prana) to move, the thought moves the pranic body, which draws the physical body. Prana is breathed into the body with the air and penetrates every cell. Without prana there is no movement, no thought, no life. Yoga Nidra helps us to increase our

When we practice Hatha yoga, we are working with both the anna maya kosha and prana maya kosha. The meridians used in acupuncture are formed where these two koshas cross. When there is a block to the flow of energy in the pranic body, it is reflected in the physical body as illness, pain, or disease. Hatha yoga enables us to work on the subtle systems of the body, keeping our energy flowing and producing health and vitality.

Mano Maya Kosha

Mano maya kosha is the body of our thoughts and senses. The subtle body where our feelings, desires, doubts, and fears live. The mano maya kosha is the storehouse for all our emotional upsets and injuries. You may be able to see scars on the physical body, but we all have emotional scars that can't be seen with the eye. The mind and body are each a manifestation of the other. What you think and feel affects the body, and what affects the body affects the mind. After an operation we spend a lot of time healing the physical body but not a lot of thought is given to healing the mental or emotional body. Yoga Nidra is a way to complete, deep, and permanent healing.

Yoga Nidra helps us to release pent-up emotions.

storehouse of energy; it literally recharges our batteries. When we feel tired, we might say, "I have no energy today." This really is true—our energy levels are depleted and need to be replenished.

Vijnana Maya Kosha

This is the subtle body of higher wisdom, where our intellect and intuition reside. When the calls of the physical body or the desires of the mind do not distract us, we can access this subtle body of higher wisdom. In our day-to-day lives we seldom hear, listen to, or trust the voice of intuition. We are more likely to do what others do, or follow the advice we have read in a book. Learn to listen to your voice of natural knowing. With the stillness that comes from the practice of Yoga Nidra, we can begin to access our higher wisdom—pure thoughts that are not affected by the ego with its feelings, desires, dislikes, expectations, and disappointments. At this level you have the experience of observing, or witnessing, the thoughts passing through the mind. The thoughts are few and pass slowly; there dawns an awareness that the "true you" is something other than these passing thoughts, which are not permanent and therefore not real.

Hatha yoga draws on both anna maya kosha and prana maya kosha.

Ananda Maya Kosha

This is the body of bliss, or joy. Here we are not distracted by and have gone beyond the body, breath, and mind. There is just the experience of peace, bliss, and contentment. It is considered blissful because you are completely detached from the situations and circumstances of your daily life. Rich or poor, healthy or sick, likes and dislikes—none of these exist in this blissful place. This is where we reside in deep, dreamless sleep. Many people refer to it as unconsciousness, a place where "nothing" is going on. However, this is not true. If it were so, how would you know that you had had a good night's sleep or that you had had a restless, disturbed night's sleep? It is only "nothing" relative to all the "things" that go on in our day-to-day lives. In Yoga Nidra you may only glimpse this bliss, but it is enough to create a real shift in the way you experience yourself, others, and the world around you. Keep practicing yoga and you will deepen the experience.

Most of us have had a glimpse of this bliss—perhaps in a moment when we experience the beauty of a sunset, before the mind starts to judge and compare it with other sunsets. Bliss is that moment of just being present to what is. When you laugh, for a split second there is no judgment or analysis; when you cuddle a newborn baby, for a moment there is complete peace and contentment. What would life be like if, instead of a fleeting moment, we could experience all of life from this place of bliss? There are people who do—we call them Sages, Gurus, or Saints.

At the very center or core of these five veils of illusion, we reach what the yogis call samadhi—the eighth and final step of Raja yoga (see chapter 3). This is where the atman, or spirit, dwells.

If you want to know God, transcend the ego. What is the ego? The mind. You could say that the mind is a collective term for the ego, thoughts, feelings, and will. When the mind is purified and clear, it can reflect your true self—your higher self. That is the goal of all spiritual paths and religions, whether Catholic or Protestant, Buddhist or Jew, Muslim or Hindu. However, you do not have to have faith in God, or in any organized religion, to experience the peace

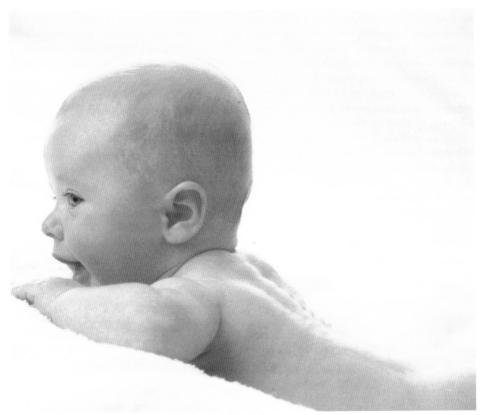

A newborn baby is free from likes and dislikes, opinions, judgments, and ego.

and bliss of your higher self. It is simply another level of consciousness. Daily, we function at a lower level of consciousness. This is the world of duality with its pleasure and pain, profit and loss. It is possible to transcend this experience of life to a higher consciousness. Instead of experiencing diversity and duality you will experience unity, unconditional love, peace, and bliss.

In yoga, this is what we mean by God. This experience is available to everyone—the first step is to get rid of selfishness. Learn to steady and purify the mind and realize the real goal of life—peace and bliss.

The next three sections of this book will provide you with a variety of practices to continue the wonderful journey that you have already begun.

Yoga Nidra

There are many deep relaxation techniques on the "market" today. This one was taught to me as part of my Integral Yoga® teacher's training. It is based on the yogic practice of pratyahara (sense withdrawal), which is the fifth limb of Raja yoga (see chapter 3) and pratyahara (see chapter 7).

During the Yoga Nidra, you will relax the physical body, bringing it and your various levels of energy into balance and being drawn deeper inward, away from the distracting body and senses. You are not sleeping, although many students do fall asleep at first. The idea is to be conscious all the way through the various stages.

do fall asleep, enjoy the rest and try to practice your Yoga Nidra at a time when you are not so sleepy. To maximize the benefits of healing and relaxing, you need to keep conscious throughout. You can, however, use it as a technique to drop off into a deep peaceful sleep if you go through the practice in bed at night.

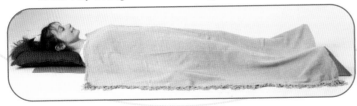

If you keep falling asleep, you can try keeping your fist slightly tensed or just touch the thumb and first finger. Some people keep an elbow bent or the eyes open or slightly open. If you start to drop off, either the falling of the arm or the movement of the eyes will wake you up. You can always practice Yoga Nidra sitting in a chair. If you

The Process

In the first stage of Yoga Nidra, you go through the body and tense the different muscle groups. When you tense the body and then let go, it releases far more tension than if you just lie there and try to relax. Lift a limb about 1 inch (2 cm) off the floor, hold it up, and squeeze it tight. At the same time, breathe in and hold the breath, forcing the prana through the body. Then let the limb flop down and the breath rush out. The limb gently hits the floor, releasing subtle tension lurking in the muscles. The release of the breath also helps to flush away deep-rooted tension. The same principle applies in car maintenance when new grease is used to flush out dirty, old grease.

This process works on the anna maya kosha. You free the body from the buildup of tension and, in the process, become more familiar with where you hold tension. With practice, you will be able to relax these areas during the day simply by telling them to "let go." You will learn what it feels like to be really relaxed, enabling you to detect tension and prevent it from building up.

If you are on your feet all day or do a lot of walking, you may feel tension in the legs or lower back. Sitting at your desk all day

Sitting at a desk all day causes tension in the body.

can cause a lot of tension in the lower back. You may have a lot of tension in the hands either from typing or from clenching your fists in stress and anxiety. This tension works its way up the arms to the shoulders. Sitting at the computer can also cause tension in the shoulders and neck, as can carrying heavy shopping bags. Worry and stress can manifest themselves in clenched teeth, which cause tension in the jaw, or frowning. Tiredness, depression, and all other feelings are expressed in the face. This first stage of Yoga Nidra enables you to free yourself from this tension, allowing the energy in the physical body to flow freely. As the physical body relaxes and you finish with movement, you experience the sensation of heaviness.

Begin with the least vital parts of the body, releasing physical tension and tense energy. Then start to draw energy and awareness in and up toward the head. After tensing and relaxing the physical body and releasing the flow of energy, go through the body mentally to release any subtle tension that remains, helping to further release tension caused by emotional upset and wounds.

In the next stage you observe the breath, working within prana maya kosha, and then the mind—mano and vijnana maya koshas. You begin to experience a deep sense of peace and stillness. With practice, you will be able to witness the breath, moving deeper within, away from the body and senses. Then you will be able to keep the awareness on the thoughts, without being wrapped up and involved in the passing drama. You will begin to experience lightness and a further distancing from the body, thoughts, and feelings. When the body and mind become calm and relaxed, prana is not needed for their movement; now you can begin to recharge your store of this vital life force.

You need to release the tension in order to restore calm to yo

The final stage is to feel the peace within. There is nothing to do but rest in the peace and enjoy it. In this place of stillness, you will know that you are not the body or mind.

After resting in this place of peace and contentment for about five minutes, slowly bring the awareness back to the breath and the body, revitalizing the system with prana. Then, slowly movement is brought back to the body. It is important to come out of the deep relaxation slowly, so all the bodies, or subtle levels of energy, are balanced and the effects of the relaxation are assimilated. You do not want to come out suddenly, disturbing the peaceful feeling.

After Yoga Nidra you will feel calm and contented; you will have freed yourself from physical tension, emotional upset, worry, and anxiety. I have seen students come out of deep relaxation and look 10 years younger! Just the other week, a new student, who suffers from panic attacks and nervous disorders, bravely came to her first class. When she arrived she looked worried and pale and had a hunched-over stance. After class she came up to me, beaming from ear to ear, with rosy cheeks and an upright posture. I couldn't believe it was the same woman!

Preparing for Deep Relaxation

Make sure you will not be disturbed for 15–20 minutes. Let your calls go to voicemail or unplug the phone.

When you first try Yoga Nidra, you may feel uncomfortable and find that it is difficult to switch off. Some people like to use relaxation music. This can help you to relax more deeply, but you want to make sure that the music is not getting in the way of you letting go completely. It may prevent you moving deeper within to experience the more subtle levels of relaxation. With practice, you will learn the art of deep relaxation without aids.

You might like to burn some incense, use scented oils, or light candles. However, make sure you put them somewhere safe. Create a relaxing atmosphere.

Make sure you are going to be warm. Cover yourself with a blanket, or wear a sweater and socks, as the body temperature will drop. A blanket will enhance the comforting, nurturing effects of the deep relaxation, helping to make you feel safe and secure.

- Lie on your back. You can lie on your bed, but it may be too easy to drop off to sleep. You may be better lying on the floor on a folded blanket or something a little soft.

- If you have a stiff neck, you may be more comfortable if you use a pillow or cushion to rest your head upon.

- If you have discomfort in the lower back, slip a cushion under the knees. Play around with the cushion to find the position that is most comfortable for you. Some people find it more comfortable to have the knees bent, feet apart, and knees resting against each other.

- The legs should be at least shoulder width apart so the legs and hips can relax. Let the feet flop out to the sides.

- The arms can be away from the body with the palms turned up to encourage the shoulders to relax down, or you can place the hands on either side of the belly.

- Keeping the head on the floor, lower the chin toward the chest to lengthen and relax the neck.

- Close the eyes.

Instructions

You can read through all the instructions given in this section and then try to go through the different stages yourself. You may find you go through the legs and arms tensing and relaxing and then the mind wanders off. If this is the case, make a recording of the instructions and play them back; this will help to keep the mind focused, making it easier to relax.

If you record the instructions, do not read the information in parentheses. Talk in a smooth, even, and gentle voice.

- After making yourself comfortable, take a couple of deep breaths. Release the air through the mouth and tell the body to let go.

- Bring the awareness to the right leg. Stretch the leg (if you tend to get cramps in the feet do not point the toes).
  Breathe in and lift the leg about an inch off the floor.

Hold the breath and squeeze the leg as tight as you can . . . tighter. (Hold for a count of 5–10.)
Let the breath rush out of the mouth and the leg flop to the floor.

- Bring the awareness to the left leg.
  Stretch the leg.
  Breathe in. Lift the leg and hold.
  Squeeze the leg as tight as you can.
  (Hold for a count of 5–10.)
  Release.

- If you like, you can roll the legs in and out, find a comfortable place for them to rest and then let them be.
  Forget about them.

- Bring the awareness to the right arm.
  Stretch the arm and spread the fingers.
  Make a tight fist.
  Breathe in and lift the arm a little.
  Hold the breath and squeeze the arm with all your strength. (Hold for a count of 5–10.)
  Release.

- Bring the awareness to the left arm.
  Stretch the arm and spread the fingers.
  Make a tight fist.
  Breathing in, lift the arm and squeeze
  as tight as you can. Hold.
  Release.

- Bring the awareness into the
  shoulders.
  Bring the shoulders up toward the
  ears, in toward the chest, and down
  toward the toes. Hold.
  Release.

- You can roll the arms in and out, find
  a comfortable place for them to rest
  and let them be.

- Now take the awareness down into
  the buttocks.
  Breathing in, tense the buttocks as
  tight as you can.
  Tighter. Hold.
  Let the breath rush out and release.

- Become aware of the belly.
  Breathing in, push the belly up like
  a balloon.

- Take in as much air as you can . . .
  a little more . . . a little more . . .
  Hold the breath (count of five), open
  the mouth and let the air rush out.

- Become aware of the chest. Breathing
  in, expand the chest. Take in a little
  more air . . . a little more . . .
  Hold.
  Relax. That's good . . . let go.

- Bring the awareness into the neck.
  Lift the head a little bit to tense the
  neck. (Hold between three to five
  seconds.)
  Relax.
  Gently roll the head from side to side
  to release any subtle tension.
  Find a comfortable place to rest the
  head and relax the neck. Let go.

- Bring the awareness into the face.
  Open the mouth and move the
  lower jaw side to side (a few times).
  Up and down.
  Open the mouth wide and stick out
  the tongue. Suck in the cheeks.
  Relax the mouth.

- Wrinkle the nose and squint the eyes.
  Relax.
  Lift the eyebrows.
  Relax.

- Finally, tense all the muscles in the
  face as tight as you can.
  Push everything forward to an imaginary
  point at the tip of the nose then . . .
  Relax.
  Feel the tension melting away as
  you let go. (Count of five.)

- Adjust your position if you need to.
  Make yourself really comfortable so
  you can remain still for the rest of the
  relaxation.

- We'll now go through the body
  mentally, so you can release any
  subtle tension that remains. (Don't
  travel through the body too quickly;
  you want to have the chance to
  detect and release any subtle tension.)
  Let the breath be natural.
  If you feel any tension, mentally and
  gently tell that part of the body to

relax, or to let go, with the
exhalation.

- Travel into the tips of the toes,
  through the feet, ankles . . . relax.

- The shins and calves, knees and
  thighs, backs of thighs . . . relax.

- Travel through the hands and wrists
  to the tips of the fingers . . . relax.

- The forearms, elbows, upper
  arms . . . relax.

- Travel into the shoulders, allowing
  them to let go and relax.

- Travel down into the buttocks . . .
  relax. Feel the hips sinking down
  toward the floor as you let go.

- Travel into the belly.
  Feel the belly becoming soft as you
  let go and relax.
  Travel up the sides of the body,
  relaxing the sides as you go.

- Come into the ribs and chest, the throat, lungs, and the heart . . . relax. Relax the heart and let go.

- Now travel down into the base of the spine . . . relax.
  Feel a wave of relaxation moving from the center of the spine and out to the sides of the body as you let go, relaxing the lower back.

- Move up to the middle of the spine . . . relax
  Relax the middle of the back.

- And then move up into the top of the spine . . . relax.
  Relax the upper back.

- Observe the entire back and allow it to relax completely.

- Travel up into the neck . . . relax.
  The jaw, tongue, and the lips . . . relax.

- Travel up into the cheeks and nose . . . eyes and ears . . . relax.
  The forehead, sides of the head,

back of the head . . . relax. (Count of three.)

- Observe the entire body and allow it to relax completely (30 seconds).

- Observe the breath, witnessing its gentle flow in and out.
  Notice how calm the breath has become (one minute).

- Now observe the mind and any thoughts passing through.
  Remain a witness.
  Simply watch the thoughts and images come and go without becoming involved in the passing drama (one minute).

- Become aware of the peace within.
  Peace—this peace is your true nature, your true self.
  Feel the peace—rest in the peace— enjoy the peace (five minutes).

- Coming out of the practice
  If you are recording, make a gentle humming sound to signal the end of

the rest period. Start softly, getting a little louder. Or you can chant "Om" (see chapter 7).

- Bring the awareness back to the breath, watching its gentle flow once again (30 seconds).

- Deepen the breathing a little and imagine you're breathing in a white, energizing light, prana, the vital life force.

- Breathe in, revitalizing the spine.

- Breathe in, energizing the vital organs, the lungs, and heart.

- Breathe in, sending the prana down through the arms and legs.

- Deepen the breath some more to energize the body and mind and begin to bring movement back into the body.

- Wiggle the fingers and toes. Gently move the face.

- Keep the breath deep and gently roll the arms and legs in and out.

- Gently roll the head from side to side.

- Still breathing deeply, revitalize and rejuvenate the entire system.

- If you want, you can gently stretch the body. Then, if you like, roll over onto your side as if you were curled up in bed. Giving yourself a little hug, know that all is well.

- Feeling peaceful, calm, and refreshed, carefully sit up when you are ready.

- There is no rush. Take your time and come into a comfortable seated position. Finish recording.

- Don't jump up to get on with "things" straight away. Take a few moments to sit quietly. Feel how calm and centered you have become.

The complete Yoga Nidra session should take about 15 minutes. You can practice it any time of day, but if you can do a little Yoga Nidra after your Hatha yoga session it helps the body to heal, assimilating the benefits of the postures, increases your energy, and gives you time to further calm the mind.

After the Yoga Nidra, if you have time, spend 15 minutes practicing pranayama (see chapter 6) and then sit for five minutes of silent meditation (see chapter 7).

Hatha yoga postures, Yoga Nidra, pranayama, and meditation form a complete system for overall health and well-being. However, only do what you comfortably have time to do. It may be that you practice your postures, do five minutes of breathing techniques, and sit for one minute of meditation, then practice your Yoga Nidra later on in the day when you have more time.

Work out a practice plan that you can stick to regularly. Two rounds of Sun Worship, one breathing technique, and one minute of sitting quietly will bring benefits to the body, emotions, and mind. Start with something small and achievable. You will feel so great that you will naturally begin to lengthen the time you spend each day getting rid of tension, increasing your energy, and calming the mind. Slowly build a regular practice that becomes part of your daily routine. Turn your practice into a habit like brushing your teeth.

6

Pranayama
(Breathing Practices)

Pranayama

> "There is no life without breath —
> to half breathe is to half live."

Sri Swami Satchidananda

Pranayama helps us to enrich the blood with oxygen, which is essential for overall health and vitality. Blood is "rich" when it contains the necessary levels of oxygen and nutrients. Therefore, you can enrich the blood through proper respiration and digestion. Pranayama can restore health and vitality to respiratory and digestive functions. It helps to improve the appetite and purifies the system by burning up toxins. Toxins are anything that the system does not want or cannot use. They can come from the food we eat and drink (see chapter 8), drugs, air pollution, and emotions such as fear or anger.

Slow, deep breathing allows the heart to rest.

Pranayama helps to boost the immune system and fight infection. When you breathe deeply, the thymus gland, situated in the upper part of the chest behind the breastbone, is massaged and stimulated, restoring proper function. The thymus gland is part of the lymphatic system—the body's waste-disposal system. The thymus produces lymphocytes. They form part of the body's white blood cells, surrounding and attacking invading agents or toxins.

Breathing deeply massages the heart, bringing health, vitality, and physical and

Pranayama cleans and strengthens the respiratory system, helping to reduce symptoms of hay fever.

emotional healing. The heart rests between beats, so when you slow the breath down the heart doesn't beat as fast, giving it more time to rest.

Pranayama calms and purifies the nervous system. When you take a long, slow exhalation, the parasympathetic nervous system is stimulated, triggering the body's natural relaxation response. It switches off the stress responses from the sympathetic system, which are switched on by stressful situations. Pranayama also helps us to relax the skeletal muscles.

Pranayama helps asthma and other respiratory disorders. It can also help to reduce the symptoms of hay fever and sinusitis by getting rid of excess mucus.

In yoga, the asanas help to give us control over the physical body and pranayama helps us to gain control over the mind, drawing the awareness inward. The breath is the link between the body and the mind, bringing them into harmony with each other. The breath reflects your state of mind. When you change your breathing patterns, you also change your mental and emotional makeup. The breath accelerates and becomes short when the mind is agitated. It slows and deepens when the mind is calm.

The Breathing Process

Electrical messages are sent from the brain, via the nervous system, to the muscles of the rib cage and the diaphragm. The diaphragm is a large, dome-shaped muscle that separates the chest cavity from the abdominal cavity. Stimulated by electrical impulses, these muscles contract, moving the ribs up and outward and contracting the diaphragm, which flattens and moves downward. The chest cavity increases, causing a slight suction and making the lungs expand. This creates a vacuum in the lungs, lowering the pressure inside, and air is drawn into the lungs to equalize the pressure. When we breathe out, the electrical messages stop, the muscles relax, and the elasticity of the lungs causes them to shrink, expelling the air.

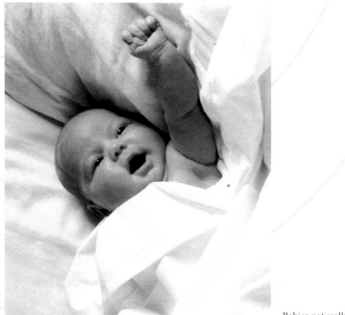

Babies naturally use deep-belly breathing.

Types of Breathing

Abdominal or Diaphragmatic Breathing

When encouraging students to breathe fully and deeply a yoga teacher might say, "breathe into the belly," or "take a deep breath, expanding the belly." You are not actually breathing into the belly, but it is a useful image. When the diaphragm contracts and flattens, the abdominal organs are pushed outward as air is drawn into the bottom of the lungs. Diaphragmatic, abdominal, or stomach breathing is known as the "Primary Breath." It is our basic method of breathing; babies only use deep-belly breathing, which develops the base of the lungs where there is a large concentration of alveoli, or air sacs.

Thoracic Breathing

When a baby is between nine months and one year old, the muscles between the ribs develop. They start to expand and contract the chest. The baby can now perform thoracic breathing, which uses the muscles of the rib cage and the midsection of the lungs. Breathing is taken away from the belly, or the lower part of

Unexpressed emotion can block deep breathing.

the lungs. As the ribs expand up and out, air is drawn in.

Along with our physical development, we are developing emotionally. The solar plexus area is known as the seat of the emotions. (Place a fist over the sternum in the center of the chest; here there is a large plexus of nerves that becomes tense through emotional upset.) Unexpressed emotion causes a block to deep abdominal breathing, limiting our intake of vital oxygen and impairing our respiratory function.

Clavicular Breathing

This uses the apex of the lungs, which extends from just under the collarbones to the sternum, and is seldom used in normal breathing. With clavicular, or upper chest, breathing, the collarbones rise up slightly. This pulls and massages the sub-clavicular muscles under the collarbones and helps to further lift the chest. Under the left sub-clavicular muscle, the lymphatic system collects toxins, breaks them down, and puts them back into the system for elimination. When we breathe into the apex of the lungs, we are helping to further purify the body's waste. With clavicular breathing we are also getting rid of stale, lifeless, residual air.

Modern society, with its fashions for tight-fitting clothes and flat stomachs, encourages shallow breathing. Military training, incorrect singing coaching, and slumped posture all create poor breathing. With the practice of yogic breathing techniques, we can relearn to breathe correctly. This will gradually help us to release unexpressed emotion with the breath and increase our health and vitality.

Prana

As you can see, there are many, many reasons for learning to breathe fully and deeply. However, with pranayama, we are not just dealing with the breath and oxygen. On a subtle level, we are dealing with prana.

> *Pra* = first
> *Na* = energy
> *Yama* = control

Prana is our vital life force; it forms the building blocks for the entire universe. In pranayama, we are restraining and controlling this vital life force. For the yogi, the body is a representation of the entire cosmos. The material used to build the universe also builds the human body. The vibration or hum of the universal energy is no different from the force that pulsates through the body. At our fundamental level, we are all nothing but energy—primordial, cosmic, conscious, energy—prana.

On the physical level, prana is seen as motion and action and on a subtle level as thought. The vibration of prana causes the mind to think; it is the energy of the mind. When the vibration is irregular, the thoughts are irregular; when our stores of prana are depleted, we cannot think clearly or concentrate properly. With the practice of pranayama, we increase, restrain, and regulate the prana, bringing harmony to this vibration, which in turn produces calm in the mind and thoughts. In chapter 2, we looked at the goal of yoga. Control the mind and you can attain enlightenment or cosmic consciousness. Control and regulation of the breath is an effective way to develop control over the mind.

Practicing pranayama regulates the pranic vibration within the body's cells. When the cells work in unison, they bring harmony and therefore health to the entire system. Prana can be directed by our thoughts. With the regular practice of pranayama, this healing energy can be stored and transmitted by thought to others in need. Through the touch, or simply by placing a hand over a sick body, healing can occur. In healing, even distance healing, energy is directed, or moved, from one place to another.

When we look at how we breathe and the benefits of oxygen-rich blood, we are concerned with the anatomy of the anna maya kosha. Here we are concerned with the anatomic aspect of the prana maya kosha. We are dealing with the subtle pranic body, which is made up of subtle astral tubes called nadis. It is estimated that there are between 72,000 and 3,000,000 nadis, which feed the body and mind with prana. The pranic body feeds the physical body and the two mental bodies—mano maya and vijnana maya kosha.

As well as obtaining prana from the air we breathe, we can charge ourselves with prana from the food we eat and drink (see chapter 8), from sunlight, and from water. Prana is at its highest if we are in the fresh air, near moving water. Prana is dissipated by "too muchness"—too much eating, eating too quickly, eating the wrong things, too much sleeping, working, talking, watching television, being too hot, too cold . . . Everything we do uses prana and too much of anything strips us of our vitality. What little prana we have left is all too often used up in uncontrolled, emotional outbursts. Notice how draining it is when you have an argument, you feel tired, and you can't think straight. For most of us, our store of prana is depleted and never recharged due to our lifestyle and improper breathing.

The physical body uses a large amount of our pranic store, which doesn't leave a lot, if anything, for mental activity, let alone spiritual development. If we try to control the mind to meditate, there is no prana to develop this control, so all we do is sit and think! When we practice pranayama, we generate this vital life force. Then, when we meditate, prana moves up for higher purposes. We don't lie down to meditate because energy is dissipated. When we sit with the spine erect, the spiritual energy that lies dormant at the base of the spine begins to rise up, just like heat.

Taking time out to relax and enjoy nature can help to replenish our store of vital energy.

The Chakras

Prana travels around the energy body through a network of subtle
energy channels called nadis. The points where the nadis cross are
called chakras. There are three main nadis—ida, pingala, and the
sushumna. The ida and pingala wrap around the sushumna, which
corresponds to the center of the spinal cord in the physical body. The
points at which the ida and pingala cross are known as the major
chakras. Chakras are energy centers, swirling vortexes of energy.
The seven main chakras correspond to nerve plexuses and endocrine
glands in the physical body. The practice of the asanas in chapter 4
will help to bring balance to the energy body. As you practice the
postures that relate to the particular chakras, you will also be
bringing health and vitality into the corresponding glands and
nerve plexuses.

Ida is associated with the moon, left,
negative, feminine, creative, intuitive,
compassionate, caring, relaxing, heart
aspects of our being, while pingala is
associated with the sun, right, masculine,
rational, logical, assertive, dispassionate,
head aspects of our being. When we
breathe in, we stimulate the sympathetic
nervous system, bringing us to action and
stimulating the pingala. When we breathe
out, we stimulate the parasympathetic
nervous system, which helps us to relax

and stimulates the ida. Hatha yoga
postures and pranayama can help us to
bring these two aspects into balance.
When this happens, a point in the middle
of the base chakra begins to open.

According to yogic philosophy, everyone
has a store of spiritual energy lying dormant
at the base of the spine, at the point of the
muladhara, or base chakra. This is often
referred to as the kundalini—a coiled
serpent, or snake, that rises up and travels
through the sushumna, piercing the major

chakras, when we begin to develop spiritually. As the chakras open, we enhance various qualities and abilities associated with the particular centers. The opening of the chakras can also bring spiritual experience. The three lower centers are associated with the earth, while the higher centers are associated with heaven. We want to bring balance and harmony so that we can experience heaven on earth.

Some schools of yoga are concerned with awakening this energy in order to experience the so-called "powers" or siddhis. However, if the kundalini is awakened prematurely, before the physical, mental, and emotional body has been strengthened and purified, it can cause mental and nervous disorders. It is far better to develop, balance, and purify gradually and to be of service, letting whatever develop as and when you are ready. The development of spiritual experience and accomplishments should not be the goal of your practice. They are simply a by-product. My Guru, Swami Satchidananda, taught that the goal should be to develop a healthy, easeful body, a calm and peaceful mind, and a happy,

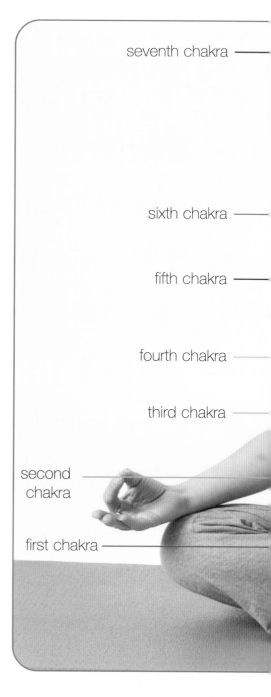

seventh chakra

sixth chakra

fifth chakra

fourth chakra

third chakra

second chakra

first chakra

useful life. Furthermore, to share what you know in order to bring health and happiness to others.

In explaining the different chakras, I refer to three qualities of nature called the gunas: sattva (purity), rajas (activity), and tamas (inertia). Everything in the manifest universe is made from these qualities, with one predominating (see chapter 8).

1 Muladhara Chakra
(Base Chakra)

Corresponds to, is associated with, and is balanced by:

- body — coccyx (at the base of the spine)
- endocrine gland — ovaries and testes
- sense — smell
- emotion — fear (most basic emotion)
- quality — centering
- development — survival
- color — red
- element — earth
- mantra — lam
- asanas — cobra, half and full locust, bow, forward bends

Our strongest instinct is to survive. We have a need to find food, shelter, clothing, or warmth. Our survival is threatened if any of these basic needs are not met. Our base survival instinct is a tamasic quality—we must survive and secure shelter at any cost. When we have enough food and a place to keep us warm, we then want our food to be tasty, to have treats, to make our home comfortable, to get a better home—this is functioning from the muladhara chakra from a rajastic quality. Many people stay at this level. They no longer fear for their basic survival, instead fear is caused by other people—the fear that someone might steal what you have, that your business might go bust or the house might burn down. The insurance industry is based on an imbalance in the first chakra! Anxiety and fear is caused by trying to hold on to what you've got. "Fear of thirst when the well is full!" When in balance, in a sattvic aspect, the chakra is open, the energy can flow through and there is no fear.

2 Svadhisthana Chakra
(Sacral Chakra)

Corresponds to, is associated with, and is balanced by:

· body	sacrum
· endocrine gland	adrenals
· sense	taste
· emotion	passion
· quality	flow
· development	family ties
· color	orange/ocher
· element	water
· mantra	vam
· asanas	half spinal twist, triangle pose

The second chakra is concerned with procreation. Nature's second strongest force is to ensure the survival of the species. Once our survival is taken care of, we procreate. At the tamasic level this is just about the continuation of the species. Developing a little, from a rajasic aspect, we bring in romance, dinner by candlelight, flowers, etc. The advertising industry is predominantly based in the second chakra.

When the second chakra is open, we have creativity. Artists, musicians, and anyone who is creative come from the second chakra in a sattvic form. Don't suppress this natural procreative force or your life will lack fulfilment. Be creative and the instinct will be satisfied.

Health problems caused from an imbalance and obstruction to the flow of energy in this center include prostate and ovarian diseases, PMS, infertility, and sexually transmitted diseases.

3 Manipura Chakra
(Solar Plexus Chakra)

Corresponds to, is associated with, and is balanced by:

- body — lumbar region of spine opposite navel, organs of digestion
- endocrine gland — pancreas
- sense — sight
- emotion — anger
- quality — activity
- development — worldly power
- color — yellow/gold
- element — fire
- mantra — ram
- asanas — bow, forward bends, yoga mudra, three-part breath

Once our survival and the survival of the species have been taken care of, we begin to look at who we are, how we relate to the rest of the world, and how it relates to us. The third chakra is concerned with power. Many modern-day diseases are associated with this center, including ulcers, liver, gallbladder and spleen problems, diabetes, immune diseases, and social diseases, such as alcoholism and physical, emotional, and mental abuse.

If you have real, sattvic power, you don't have to show or assert it. When power is tamasic, we aren't aware of it; when power is rajasic we use it to get more power. If we are not naturally powerful, we can create bad power and use it out of the first and second charkas. This is the origin of physical abuse and violence—using power to overcome fear and passion. Lack of self-esteem, feeling bad about yourself, can lead to attempts to dominate and gain power over others. When feeling disempowered, people may also have a tendency to overeat—third chakra reflecting on the first. Habitual behavior—smoking, drugs, drinking, overeating—stem from the third chakra. We feel powerless, so our habits have power over us.

Teachers, therapists, and professors come from the third chakra. If it is not purified, they tend to make a lot of money but provide little service.

Angry children are usually very intelligent and should be given respect. They need to be given freedom and to be empowered; otherwise the anger can lead to hate, which can lead to self-hate. Don't try to break angry children; the power in them needs to be tamed and channeled, so give them direction and let go.

When the third chakra is purified and energy is flowing through, we get powerful and benevolent leaders—people like Mahatma Ghandi and Martin Luther King, Jr. When using power in its sattvic form, we bring benefit and no harm. The most powerful power is hidden, benevolent spiritual power. To purify yourself, in order to develop and use power for the benefit of humanity, start serving others selflessly.

Feeding people is reflecting on the first chakra and providing shelter is reflecting on the second.

The first three chakras are the lower, earth chakras. Above the third chakra, there is a huge knot, or nerve ganglion, that makes it very difficult to move from the lower earth centers to heaven. It is from these chakras that we get the negative emotions of fear, passion, and anger; there are no negative emotions associated with the higher centers. In order to purify the third center, engage yourself in Karma yoga—selfless service—and keep up the other practices to purify body and mind. By serving others, we can start to purify the three lower chakras and begin to move our energy up.

4 Anahata Chakra
(Heart Chakra)

Corresponds to, is associated with, and is balanced by:

· body	heart and lungs
· endocrine gland	thymus
· sense	touch
· emotion	love
· quality	feeling
· development	compassion
· color	pink/green
· element	air
· mantra	yam
· asanas	cobra, fish, bow, shoulder stand, chanting, laughter, love.

Love is perceived in the first three chakras, but here we are talking about divine, unconditional love. To be more precise, we are talking about compassion. Once the fourth chakra is open, we lose our sense of individual family. From the first three chakras we would say, "I love you because . . ." From the fourth chakra love is like sunshine—it's for everyone. Everyone is our family, we love all equally, and we love because we are love. Everyone can love from this center, but the love will manifest through the center where we are most dominant, i.e. love of the home and security, sex, or power. When the anahata chakra is open, the whole world changes; even the ugliest, most impure thing becomes beautiful.

Problems in our physical health can arise when we are not loved enough, or we do not love enough. What little opening there is in the heart center, we try to keep closed. This can lead to problems and, in some cases, major disease of the lungs, heart, and thymus gland (leading to immune deficiency, AIDS, and some cancers). The main problem for the heart is the feeling of isolation; the more alone we feel, the more the heart center closes, arteries harden and clog, cutting circulation to the heart and increasing the sense of isolation. Poor circulation and lack of prana also closes the heart. Develop love and compassion through selfless service. Don't serve because you think you should—this is coming from the third chakra—serve because you can. The more you give, the more you will receive.

Laughter is a social medicine and one of the best remedies for heart patients. It releases emotional upset and blocked energy, encouraging its upward flow from the third to the fourth chakra. Laughter can help to release endorphins into the blood stream, producing a natural high. It can free you from the physical manifestations of stress by the release of muscle-relaxing hormones. Laughter also boosts and builds our immunity by increasing the "T" cells in the blood. So go ahead, laugh—even if you have to fake it until you make it!

5 Vishuddha Chakra
(Throat Chakra)

Corresponds to, is associated with, and is balanced by:

- body   cervical spine (base of throat)
- endocrine gland   thyroid
- sense   hearing
- emotion   we are beyond emotion (this chakra is concerned with communication.)
- quality   introspection
- development   self-analysis
- color   blue
- element   space
- mantra   ham
- asanas   cobra, shoulder stand, fish, spinal twist

This is the highest point where the ida and pingala cross. A higher understanding of nature and people begins to develop. Energy is balanced. Clairvoyance—the ability to predict or to see the future—also develops.

Concerned with communication when open in this chakra, you will monitor your speech. Speech should be truthful, tranquil, beneficial, and pleasant. When open in the throat, chakra speech never causes harm—it is divine communication.

Blockage to the flow of energy in the fifth chakra, a lack of purity, can lead to throat, sinus, ear, and mouth problems. To develop purity be silent and listen. We have two ears that are always open and one mouth, which is naturally shut! Don't waste your energy in idle gossip. The truly wise person listens and speaks little.

The opening of the throat chakra brings a developed intellect. The ability to read anything and to understand it immediately is the highest intellect.

6 Ajna Chakra
(Eyebrow Chakra or Third Eye)

Corresponds to, is associated with, and is balanced by:

- body — brain
- endocrine gland — pituitary
- sense — thought
- quality — focus
- development — wisdom
- color — indigo/silver
- element — beyond the elements
- mantra — om
- asanas — eye movements, shoulder stand, fish, headstand, nadi suddhi, alternate nostril breathing, chanting om

We are now concerned with wisdom. When the ajna chakra is open, we go beyond brotherly and sisterly divine love. We are beyond body and personality. We are just knowledge—total, complete, pure, wisdom. We are beings of light and not a physical body. It would be difficult to live and function in the world if coming purely from the sixth chakra. You would just see light and not be aware of the physical body. We don't think from the ajna chakra; we know. There is no emotion—wisdom does not have emotion, it just is.

7 Sahasara Chakra
(Crown Chakra)

Corresponds to, is associated with, and is balanced by:

- body — crown of the head
- endocrine gland — pineal
- sense — intuition
- quality — ananda—bliss
- development — spirituality
- color — pure white/violet
- mantra — silence
- asanas — eye movements, shoulder stand, fish, headstand, nadi suddhi, chanting om

There is nothing to say. This is the final state of self-realization, samadhi—pure bliss. When the energy goes up to the crown chakra, you are beyond the body and mind. The energy stays up and leaves the body—there is no more self.

You can attain samadhi—the goal of yoga—from the opening and purifying of any of the chakras from the heart up.

When practicing asanas, pranayama, and meditation, it helps to control the mind if you focus the awareness on one of the chakra centers. To develop purity and spiritual qualities and to overcome our more base tendencies, it is advisable to focus on one of the higher centers. You can repeat one of the mantras or use the colors associated with the centers. You may find that when concentrating on a particular center you see a different color—that's fine go with that. Go with your own experience and enjoy the ride!

A lotus flower, each with a different number of petals, symbolically represents each chakra. You can focus on the chakra and visualize the lotus flower closed and pointing downward. You then visualize the flower turning around to point up and see it

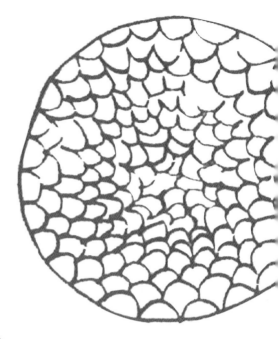

opening up and blossoming, allowing the energy to flow through. This is a lovely visualization to do at the anahata chakra, the heart center.

Muladhara—four petals
Svadhisthana—six petals
Manipura—ten petals
Anahata—twelve petals
Vissudha—sixteen petals
Ajna—two petals
Sahasara—infinite

The safest and surest way to develop spiritually, to ensure the awakening of your spiritual energy and the purifying of your chakras is through service. "The keynote of yoga is dedication. It is the master key to all joy and peace. This is the basic teaching of Yoga and all religions: give, give, give. Let every minute of your life be useful to humanity. Bring peace and joy to everybody and no harm to anybody. This is the only way to true happiness; there are no shortcuts." Sri Swami Satchidananda.

Pranayama Practice

When it comes to yoga, it is said that an ounce of practice is worth a ton of theory! Theory over, let's get on with learning some breathing techniques that will help to transform your life.

- Sit in a comfortable position. You can cross the legs or kneel. If you prefer, use a cushion. You can sit with the back against a wall or use a chair (see chapter 4). You want to be able to sit still, so there is no wastage of prana. The body needs to be relaxed and warm. If there is tension or you are cold or too hot you will waste prana and the mind will be distracted.

- Keep the spine erect, the chest well spread out, and the shoulders down. This will enable you to lift and expand the chest as you develop and use the full capacity of your lungs. If you sit with a slumped posture, the chest cannot expand properly in deep breathing and strain is caused to the system.

- If you feel uncomfortable, light-headed, or dizzy at any time, stop the practice and return the breath to normal.

- Always begin any new technique in yoga gently and cautiously, particularly the breathing practices. You are dealing with the delicate organs of the lungs, heart, and the nervous system, so do not strain. If you find yourself breathing in or out with a gasp or sigh, you are beginning to strain. Adjust what you are doing.

- Unless stated otherwise, the breathing techniques always begin with an exhalation and breathing is done through the nose. Breathing through the nose filters and warms the air. It gives us greater control over the breath, prana, and mind. It also helps to improve the flow of energy through the ida and pingala.

- The exception is the Cleansing Breath, where you breathe in through the nose and let the air rush out of the mouth with a sigh. This is a great technique to use between postures. It helps to release toxins, unexpressed emotion, and tension.

Deergha Swaasm
(Deep Three-part Breathing)

This technique teaches you how to use the full capacity of your lungs through abdominal, thoracic, and clavicular breathing. You will take in seven times more oxygen than with normal, shallow breathing, bringing all the benefits associated with deep breathing and rich, oxygenated blood.

You are going to be breathing in three parts. It sounds quite easy. However, due to years of incorrect breathing, many of us perform what is known as "reversed breathing." Instead of the belly extending out with an inhalation, it contracts and is pulled in. To learn the technique properly, try these steps first.

1

Place your hands on your belly. Exhale. As you inhale, feel the belly expand. Exhale and feel the belly contract. This is abdominal breathing. Practice it for a few breaths.

Check that you have not developed reversed breathing. Make sure the belly goes out with an inhalation and in on an exhalation, i.e. the belly is moving the opposite way of the breath.

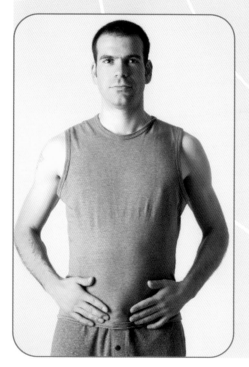

2

Place your hands either side of the ribs, fingers pointing toward the center of the body. Exhale. Inhale and feel the ribs expand as they lift up and out. This is thoracic breathing using the midsection of the lungs. Practice for a few breaths.

3

Place the fingers over the collarbones. Exhale. Inhale and see if you can feel the upper chest rising slightly. This is clavicular breathing and you are breathing right up into the apex of the lungs. Practice for a few breaths.

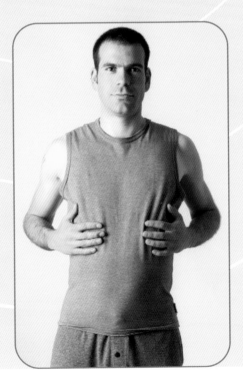

When you have got the hang of the three different parts, you can join them together to form one slow, smooth and even breath—inhaling and expanding from the bottom to the top (filling a jug), exhaling and contracting from the top to the bottom (emptying a jug).

1

Sit comfortably, with the spine erect and the shoulders down. Close the eyes.

2

Exhale. Inhale, expanding the belly, ribs, and upper chest.

3

Exhale as the upper chest sinks, the ribs come in, and the belly contracts. Gently pull the belly in as you finish the exhalation to empty the lungs as much as possible. This way you will be able to take in more fresh air on the inhalation.

Practice for three minutes. To help you concentrate, you can count the breath. Over time you will be able to increase your lung capacity and your count will increase. Take it slowly—there's no rush.

Deep Three-part Breathing in Daily Life

This is a great technique to use if you become emotionally upset, overexcited, or stressed. Remember that the breath calms the mind, soothes the emotions, and helps you to relax.

Rather than getting into a heated argument, take a few slow, deep breaths and allow yourself to calm down before you open your mouth. If you are unable to speak properly because you are upset and/or crying, again take a few slow, deep

Three-part breathing helps you stay focused all day.

breaths, allow the thoughts to slow and calm and the emotions to settle. If you are irritated, angry, afraid, or nervous, use the same technique—deep, slow breaths stimulate the parasympathetic nervous system and will help you to think clearly, relax, and calm down.

When you are breathing deeply, bring the awareness to the breath. You can do this by:

1
Watching the breath at the tip of the nose. Notice the cool, calming air coming in and the warm, stressed air going out.

2
You can watch the movement of the body as you breathe.

3
Notice the length of the exhalation to the inhalation.

4
Simply count the breath.

Deep breathing helps to manage pain and heal the body. Breathe into the pain. Imagine the prana is dissolving the discomfort or replacing the diseased cells. You can imagine a color, white, energizing light, cool water, a fresh breeze, or anything that comes to your mind.

Breathe into the affected area and, as you exhale, imagine you are washing, blowing, or breathing away the pain, discomfort, or illness.

Some people like to imagine the prana collecting up and dissolving the sick cells. As they exhale, the dissolved cells are breathed away in the form of gray soot that disappears as it is breathed out through the nose. You can use this technique to help get rid of anxiety or headaches, period pain, and more serious illnesses that are affecting the body and mind.

Brahmari
(Humming Bee Breath)

This is wonderful for calming the emotions and mind, bringing a sense of peace and well-being; it also helps to tone the vocal cords. The humming sound helps to focus the mind, and the vibration created helps to balance and regulate the function of the pituitary gland, which is located in the center of the head, surrounded by blood, and protected by bone. The humming makes the blood vibrate, which in turn vibrates and tones the pituitary gland. It is known as the master gland as it affects and regulates most of the other endocrine glands. The pituitary is responsible for our emotional, mental, and physical health and well-being.

1
Sit comfortably with the spine erect, the shoulders relaxed, and the eyes closed.

2
Inhale using the three-part breath.

3
Exhale slowly, making a gentle humming sound.

4
Feel the vibration on the soft palate at the center of the head and then feel the vibration moving higher. Repeat for one to three minutes.

You can play around with the key—making some high, some low. Notice where you feel the vibration when the pitch changes. If there is a particular pitch you like, stick with that.

To help bring the awareness further within you can apply Yogi Mudra. This is an energy seal that helps to focus the mind and concentrate prana, taking the awareness away from the senses.

1

Bring both hands toward the face and spread the fingers.

2

Place the thumbs in the ears, the index fingers gently over the eyes, the middle fingers on the sides of the nostrils, the ring fingers above the top lip, and the little fingers below the bottom lip.

3

Perform Brahmari as before, repeat for about five breaths, release the hands, and sit quietly. Notice how calm, still, and peaceful you have become.

Kapaalabhati
(Skull Shining Breath)

This is a rapid, diaphragmatic breathing technique that consists of short, quick, forced exhalations, followed by natural automatic inhalations. It is called the Skull Shining Breath because it cleans the nadis in the skull and enhances the complexion. This technique oxygenates the entire system, and increases energy and vitality. It's a great technique to use if you are feeling tired and you've got to keep working and concentrating. It's really useful for blowing the cobwebs away and helping you stay alert.

1

Sit comfortably with the spine erect and the shoulders down. Close the eyes.

2

To begin with, place a hand on the belly. Exhale completely.

3

Take a half breath, expanding the belly only.

4

Snapping the belly in make a quick, forced exhalation.

5

As the belly relaxes, air is automatically drawn in.

- Make sure the shoulders keep still and the face is relaxed.

- Don't strain. If your exhalations are quite loud, you are probably using too much force.

- To make sure you are not reverse breathing, place a hand on the belly. Make sure the belly is coming in as the breath comes out.

- If you find this difficult, slow down the technique. You may find it useful to gently push the belly in as you exhale.

- Make sure you take an inhalation after each exhalation. Some people keep repeating short exhalations only, eventually running out of breath.

- If you still have difficulty getting the rhythm right, try lying on your back.

- You can imagine you are trying to blow a fly off the tip of the nose! The snapping in of the abdomen is what happens naturally when you sneeze, cough, or laugh.

- Begin with three rounds of 10–15 breaths.

- With the last exhalation of each round, exhale completely and then take a deep three-part breath in and out with control. When you feel ready, begin the next round. Stick with three rounds, but you can gradually increase the number of breaths in each round.

- If you feel dizzy or light-headed, stop! Return the breath to normal.

- Do not practice this during menstruation.

Nadi Suddhi
(Nerve Purification)

This is the same as deep three-part breathing, only through alternate nostrils. Nadi Suddhi strengthens and purifies the nervous system. It balances the right and left hemispheres of the brain and helps to calm and organize the thoughts, focusing the mind.

Nadi Suddhi helps to balance the ida and pingala, bringing balance. When we are not in a state of balance, energy does not flow up the sushumna but stays in the ida or the pingala. Flushing out the ida and pingala with Nadi Suddhi is like cleaning our arteries; the flow of prana becomes thick and even as they are supplied with a river of energy, instead of a stream. This creates heat at the base of the spine, which vibrates, shaking the energy loose so it can flow up the sushumna, piercing the chakras as it rises up. Ida and pingala go up as far as the top of the nose; it is only the sushumna that goes right up to heaven, opening the ajna and sahasarara chakras.

1. Sit comfortably with the spine erect, shoulders relaxed, and eyes closed.

2. Bend either elbow and make a gentle fist with the hand. From the fist release the thumb and the last two fingers. This is Vishnu Mudra (see chapter 4).

3. Exhale. Inhale, using the three-part breath, and gently close the right nostril with the thumb, if you are right-handed, or the fingers if you are left-handed.

4. Gently exhale through the left nostril.

5. Inhale through the left and then switch. Exhale through the right, inhale and switch.

6. Continue—exhale, inhale, switch.

7. When you are comfortable with the rhythm, you can begin to count the breath. Work toward having the exhalations twice as long as the inhalations.

- Begin with a ratio of 4:8. Breathe in for a count of 4 and out for a count of 8. Work at keeping the breath smooth and even. If you suddenly have to gasp for air, your ratio is too great so adjust accordingly. Gradually you can begin to increase your ratio.

- Continue for three minutes to begin with. Stop at any time should you feel light-headed, dizzy, or in any way uncomfortable.

Using Nadi Suddhi in Daily Life

If you are tired and can't concentrate or think clearly, it can be very hard to make decisions. Practice a few rounds of Nadi Suddhi and you will find the thoughts calm and organize themselves. Try it—it works!

If you have to confront a difficult situation and are finding it hard to know what to say, practice a few rounds of Nadi Suddhi.

Nadi Suddhi is like the valve on a pressure cooker; it slowly and calmly releases pressure. If the pressure is allowed to build and build, the lid will come flying off, spraying carrots and peas everywhere! Don't let emotional upset build until you have an outburst. When the passions rise and are let loose, you are no longer rational and effective communication goes out the window. The same technique also helps to release the damaging effects caused by the buildup of fear, depression, and anxiety.

To help control the emotions and restore a calm mind, practice Nadi Suddhi three times a day, or whenever you feel the need. If you are at work or in a public place, you could sneak off to the bathroom or just do the deep three-part breath instead.

Practicing this breath can ease stress and pressure anywhere.

You can add to the technique by repeating a positive affirmation as you breathe. Anything that will inspire and have an uplifting effect on the mind, such as "I am calm, I am peaceful," or "I am courageous, I am strong" will work. Repeat one statement on the inhalation and the other on the exhalation.

Ujjayi
(Hissing Breath)

The purpose of Ujjayi is to help increase control over the breath and aid concentration, bringing the awareness inward. It is used in conjunction with the three-part breath or Nadi Suddhi.

As you inhale and exhale, gently contract the back of the throat, or epiglottis, creating a soft hissing sound. Notice the sound and friction of the air rubbing at the back of the throat. Do not make the friction too rough or the hissing too loud.

After Your
Pranayama Practice

When you have finished your breathing practices, always sit quietly for a few minutes (at least one!). The mind will be very calm and still. Give yourself an opportunity to enjoy this wonderful peace, carrying the benefits into the rest of your life.

Pranayama is the fourth step of Raja yoga and takes us from the physical practices to the mental practices of sense withdrawal, concentration, and meditation, leading to the eighth and final step of samadhi—the super-conscious state. Pranayama provides the perfect preparation for meditation.

7

Dhyana
(Meditation)

Dhyana

Meditation is keeping the mind focused on one point or object. Preparing well for meditation is as important as the meditation itself — if you prepare well, you are half done. Practicing your postures and deep relaxation helps you to get rid of tension and relax the body, enabling you to sit still without meditating on aches and pains! Pranayama begins to steady the mind and generates the energy needed for spiritual practices.

So there you sit, prepared to move into your meditation practice, when all of a sudden you hear something and the mind wanders off. Your calm and focused mind has been distracted by the organs of sense, i.e. the tongue, nose, ears, etc. Upon hearing a sound the mind starts a conversation trying to figure out what the sound is. You might smell something and again the mind will be distracted.

The first step along the way to meditation is to be able to draw the mind away from sense objects, then, with practice, you will be able to gain control over the sense organs. The sense organs themselves are harmless. The trouble begins when there is no control over them. Focused on worldly objects, the senses stimulate thoughts, feelings, emotions, and desire, making the mind restless. Once there is desire, the mind will not rest until the desire has been fulfilled. When a desire is fulfilled, the satisfaction experienced is short-lived and is soon replaced by another desire.

When we sit with the eyes closed and turn our awareness inward, the senses find peace and focus upon the stillness, or light within. The mind, no longer disturbed by the organs, or objects of sense, assumes its natural condition of peace. Withdrawing of the senses is called pratyahara and is the fifth limb of Raja yoga.

Once the mind is no longer disturbed by the body or the senses, you can begin to practice dharana (concentration), the sixth limb of Raja yoga. This is the beginning of meditation. You are training the mind to stay fixed upon one object, or in one place. When the mind becomes fixed upon one object and no other thoughts pop up, you are meditating, or practicing dhyana, the seventh limb of Raja yoga.

Try some of the techniques in this chapter. You will find that as soon as you try to keep the mind focused on one thing, another thought springs into the mind, which calls another and then another. Before you know it, you've forgotten about the object of meditation. For example, you may try to practice the gazing technique, or tratak (see page 206). You may decide to gaze at a candle. Gazing at the candle, a thought pops up about the lovely candlelit dinner you had last week. Then you think about the food that you ate, then you might think, "what will I eat tonight?" then "I'll have to go to the supermarket; I hope I'll be able to park" . . . the mind has jumped from candle to car parking spaces, probably within a minute!

When you notice the mind has wandered, gently bring it back to the candle. This process of bringing the mind back once it has wandered off is concentration. When the mind stays fixed, it is meditation. When you can remain in a meditative state for an extended period of time, you can attain samadhi, the super-conscious state. This is when the meditator and the object of meditation become one. In concentration, you are making the effort; in meditation there is no sense of effort, you are just there. There is the object, the meditator, and the meditation. In samadhi there is no you or object—everything is One, there is no sense of "I," just peace and bliss.

The gazing technique helps to steady the mind.

Why Meditate?

Meditation helps us attain enlightenment. However, there are also many interim benefits from a regular meditation practice. Meditation has been clinically proven to reduce high blood pressure, improve the body's natural immunity, and increase vitality.

You will begin to feel stronger and calmer as you develop mental and emotional balance and stability. You will be able to deal with difficult situations with greater control and recover from upset much more quickly. Emotional stress will not affect you as much. You will be able to think more clearly, concentrate more deeply, and your memory will improve.

With regular meditation you will feel more contented with life, which will seem to make more sense. It becomes easier to make choices and to follow the correct path of action with a sense of being in control of your life.

Meditation is a great stress-management technique, a perfect antidote for today's hectic, stressful lifestyle.

Create a "meditation space" with objects to calm or uplift the mind.

Developing a Practice

The most important thing is to have a regular practice. In *The Yoga Sutras* Patanjali says, "Practice becomes firmly grounded when well attended to for a long time, without break and in all earnestness."

Today we are used to having things instantly—food, money—so why not enlightenment? Sorry, it doesn't work like that! Patanjali doesn't say how long, he just says it takes a long time. Forget how long you've been practicing; just know that you're on the right path and that sooner or later you will get there.

The second criterion for practice is that it is without break—continuous, regular practice—until it becomes more important than anything else. Some people say, "I've been meditating for years, but I still don't seem to be getting anywhere." Then, you discover that they may have been meditating for several years, but there has been nothing regular about the practice—every day one week, nothing the next, two days the following week and so on.

It is important to develop regular practice if you are to maximize the benefits gained by meditating.

The third criterion for practice is that you meditate in all earnestness. Some people meditate regularly, but they sit there thinking about the movie they watched on television last night or the new sports car they are saving to buy. You need to give meditation your full attention and concentration and you need to have complete faith in what you are doing.

The three qualities needed to develop your meditation practice are patience, devotion, and faith.

Start slowly and build your practice. Begin with five minutes of pranayama and then five minutes of meditation. Stick to this regularly and increase the time slowly. This way you will build a habit and find it becomes easier to meditate than to miss your practice.

The most common obstacle to developing and continuing with meditation practice is being judgmental. Don't judge your practice. The mind has a tendency to remember the bad times. There is no such thing as a "bad" meditation; it's only "bad" when you don't meditate at all. I don't mean bad in the sense that you are wrong or naughty! It's just that meditation enhances the quality of life, so for the sake of peace of mind, contentment, and fulfilment— meditate! Even if your mind is very distracted, still meditate. The mind is what it is, don't judge, just accept what is so.

There should be no expectation. Expectation will lead to disappointment. Remember you need to have patience. Try not to look upon your meditation as a means to an end but rather as an end in

itself. In other words, just meditate for the joy of meditating now and not for any expected results; meditation builds slowly over time. It's like singing—the purpose is not to get to the end, we do it because we enjoy doing it.

Distracting Thoughts

When you begin to meditate, thoughts will bubble up and distract the mind from its object of meditation. There are several ways of dealing with this.

Bring the mind back gently but firmly, as if you are training a small child to do something new. You can tell the mind, "I know you want to think about summer vacation, but right now you are meditating, you can think about the holiday later."

Try to ignore the thoughts.

Watch the thoughts come and go like the passing of clouds. Don't indulge and get involved with them. Just watch them come and go.

If it's a negative thought, try replacing it with a positive thought and then return to your object of meditation.

If you have a persistent thought, focus on the distraction and analyze it. Ask yourself, "Are the problems real?" "Is there anything I can do about it right now?" "Are these thoughts who I really am?" "If I fulfil this desire, will the satisfaction last forever?" "Will it bring me permanent peace and joy?" "Is anything more important than my ultimate goal of peace and joy?" Then, return to your object of meditation.

The Mind

Where is the mind? If you were to open your brain, would you find a mind? No. There is no such thing as a mind. The mind is a collection of thoughts, which in yoga is called chitta. One thought is called vritti.

In chapter 1 we looked at the goal of yoga:

"Yogas chitta vritti nirodha" (the restraint of the modifications of the mind stuff is yoga)

The Yoga Sutras, Book One, Sutra 2

In yoga the chitta is said to have

three parts:

ahamkara: This is the ego, the basic mind. It is where the sense of "I," "me," and "mine" comes from.

buddhi: This is the intellect, or discriminative faculty, of the mind. It is above any judgment. This is the part of the mind that identifies and is free of emotion. The Vulcans in *Star Trek* are great Buddhis!

manas: This is the part of the mind that is connected with the senses. The manas interprets messages sent to the brain from the senses; it is the desiring part of the mind.

Trying to train the mind is like a parent teaching a small child; you need to be patient, loving, and firm.

With meditation practice, we want to quiet and control the mind, or chitta. Due to the ahamkara, the mind thinks it is a real entity and the manas adds to this illusion. The mind only exists by generating thoughts; therefore meditation is a threat to its survival. You have to create a non-hostile environment for the mind. Don't get impatient and angry; remember, treat it like a small child, be loving but firm. When you first sit for your meditation practice, let the mind have a ball. Simply watch what is going on with no sense of "I" and without being judgmental. Let the mind speak up; let the thoughts have their day. Then begin to tame the mind by introducing your object of meditation. Between two thoughts there is nothing—silence. All you are trying to do is to increase that space. As the ahamkara, the sense of "I" drops away, the fear for survival drops away, and the manas becomes quiet. Slowly you prepare the mind to face the truth—that it doesn't exist, it isn't real, and it is not who you are. This is done slowly, slowly, slowly! First you reduce the thoughts and slow them down, then eventually you will just have the thought of your object of meditation, and eventually even that will drop away.

Meditation Hints

- It's best not to meditate right after a meal. Wait at least two hours. You need energy to meditate. If you've just eaten, your energy will be used for digestion. Also, if the body is heavy with food, you are likely to fall asleep.

- If you are new to meditation, do a few asanas first to get rid of toxins and tension, followed by pranayama, and then meditation.

- If you are meditating in the morning, take a cold shower or splash some cold water on your face to help fully awaken the body and mind so that you don't fall asleep during your practice.

- Make sure your clothing is comfortable and sufficiently warm because the body will cool as you relax. A blanket or shawl can easily be dropped off your shoulders if you become hot.

- Meditate in a well-ventilated room.

- If possible, have a separate room for your yoga practice. If this is not possible, see if you can find a corner or some space that you can regularly use. Decorate your meditation space with inspiring pictures, candles, incense, sacred objects, flowers, or seashells— anything that will remind you of your purpose in meditation. Remember, we want to learn to control the senses, so give them something inspiring and uplifting to play with. In that way, the messages they send to the mind will generate thoughts associated with meditation. When you practice regularly in the same room, wearing the same clothes, it develops peaceful vibrations that will help to calm the mind. If ever you feel upset or stressed, go and sit in your meditation room or space and you will feel calmed.

- As well as meditating in the same place, try to meditate at the same time each day. Two sittings daily of 15–20 minutes (you can begin with five minutes and work up) is a good start for meditation practice. Sit in the morning when you get up and in the evening before going to bed. Very early morning (4–7 AM) is an especially good time to meditate. This time is known as Brahmamuhurta; prana is at its highest, the atmosphere is very calm, the air is clean, and the vibrations are more conducive for meditation before the hustle and bustle of the day begins.

- Prepare well by doing pranayama.

Practical Considerations

- It can be helpful to schedule your practice, or sadhana, in a methodical, businesslike way. Decide the length of your meditation period the night before. Take into consideration how long it will take you to shower and get ready, and then decide what time you need to get up. Make a firm, clear contract with yourself—a sankalpa. Give your meditation priority over everything else for the contracted time. Be realistic. If five minutes is all you can do to begin with, that's fine. Stick to your contract. Don't sit for longer or shorter; you can adjust the length of time the following day.

- Don't be anxious or disturbed by the distracting thoughts that come into the mind during your sitting. Simply try to ignore them. Know that your intention is meditation. If these thoughts want to sit for a while in your mental "room," that's up to them. Don't try to force them out; you'll create an enemy. Learning to let go of these distracting thoughts is a valuable technique.

- Be loving, but firm. Don't make your mind afraid of you. After all, it's just doing the best it can under the circumstances! Let it know why you take it to meditation.

- Sometimes it may seem that your mind is more disturbed in meditation than at other times. Usually this is because you've never been still or quiet enough to notice all the "static" on your mental radio. It's always been there—it's you! Enjoy the movie or game, all the drama, romance, intrigue, and comedy; watch the show as it goes by, but don't get caught up in any of the scenes, no matter how dramatic or beautiful. Remain a witness. Use your object of meditation to anchor you in one place, like a boat in a storm.

- Practice Karma Yoga. Take care of those aspects of your life that cause the mental disturbance. Serve those around you; remember that, "The dedicated ever enjoy Supreme Peace."

- Make sure you have satsanga—company of the wise—regularly. Association with other spiritual seekers helps immensely.

- Read about the lives of saints or virtuous people who have helped humanity. Read uplifting spiritual works. The mind likes to play with facts and bits of information; give it something inspiring, uplifting, and helpful.

- Most important of all—have fun!

Meditation Techniques

In yoga, no one way of meditation is given. The criteria for choosing an object of meditation are that it should be uplifting and that the mind should enjoy it. Try out the various techniques and find out for yourself which one fulfills these criteria. Once you find a technique that works for you, stick with it. Many people use a technique for a few months and get "bored" or discouraged when they don't see bright lights! Persevere—meditation is a science, you will get results if you stick with it and go deeper and deeper into meditation. Like digging a well, there is no point in stopping before you reach water to begin another hole—you have to keep digging!

Tratak (Gazing)

"Where the eyes go the mind follows." Concentrating and meditating on a visual form is a great way to steady and control the mind. This technique helps to improve the eyesight and to stimulate the brain through the optic nerve.

You can practice tratak on a yantra. This is a mystical symbol in the form of a geometric diagram that represents a particular aspect of the divine. Yantras are experienced in deep meditation and then brought back into normal consciousness. The yantra given here is the Integral Yoga® yantra and is a representation of the entire cosmos.

yantra®

Other good objects for tratak are: the flame of a candle, a flower, sunset, a photograph of a natural scene, a picture of a saint, prophet, Guru, or an incarnation of the divine.

1

Sit comfortably, with the spine erect and the shoulders relaxed.

2

Practice without glasses or contact lenses.

3

Place your object at eye level about 3 feet (1 m) away.

4

Gently gaze at your object but be careful not to strain.

5

Gaze at the middle of the object without blinking.

6

When the eyes begin to sting or water, gently close them and visualize the image of your object in the mind's eye.

7

When the image fades, open the eyes and continue gazing.

Repeat this process for the allotted time of your meditation.

After practicing tratak for a while, developing greater control over the mind, you may find that you no longer need the physical object to gaze at. You will be able to visualize your object.

Visualization

Sitting with the eyes closed, visualize a
scene from nature, such as a tree, lake,
or mountain, a star, or the moon. You
can visualize a place where you were
particularly happy or peaceful. Visualize the
scene with as much detail as possible.

Keep bringing the mind back to your
visual image.

Mantra Japa

Mantra means that which steadies the mind; Mantra Japa is the repetition of a mantra (see chapter 4). Like yantras, mantras were realized in deep states of meditation. A mantra is a sound structure of one or more syllables that represent a particular aspect of the divine vibration. Repetition and concentration on a particular mantra can help you to develop that spiritual vibration. The repetition of a mantra is one of the most effective and simplest ways to calm the body and mind, bringing into balance our different levels of energy (see chapter 5). When you repeat a mantra, you are literally realigning yourself with the hum of the universe and bringing your vibration in line with an aspect of the divine vibration.

Mantras used in yoga are usually in Sanskrit, which is said to be the perfect language. This is because the sounds used to form the words create the vibration of the experience of that quality. For example if you repeat "Om shanti," which means peace, you will experience a peaceful vibration and manifest the qualities of peace within every cell in your body and mind.

You can receive mantra initiation and a personal mantra from a Guru or teacher.

You can repeat your chosen mantra whenever and wherever you like, not just in your formal meditation practice. Repeat your mantra until it becomes firmly rooted in the mind. When this happens, your body, breath, mind, and life begin to develop the rhythm and vibration of the mantra.

Mantras to Practice:

Hari Om

Hari is an aspect of God that removes
obstacles. Sitting comfortably with the eyes
closed, repeat "hari om" with the inhalation
and "hari om" with the exhalation. You can
try different variations, keeping the mantra
in sync with the breath. Experiment and
find out what works best for you.

HA moves energy up from the solar
    plexus area.

RI contracts the throat giving power to
    the upward movement of the
    energy.

O   opens the throat allowing the
    energy to move higher still.

M   the energy vibrates in the head.

Om Shanti

Om is the basic sound vibration of the universe that vibrates in every cell in your body. Shanti means peace. My Guru, Sri Swami Satchidananda, says:

- Repeat "Om" with the inhalation and visualize energy in the form of white light moving down the spine and striking at the base.

- Repeat "shanti" with the exhalation and visualize the energy moving up the spine to the top of the head.

- If you find it difficult to visualize the energy moving up and down the spine, you can focus on the breath at the tip of the nose as you repeat "Om" with the inhalation and "shanti" with the exhalation.

- With continuous practice, over time, you may begin to feel the flow of prana, a warm sensation moving up the spine.

"Shanthi (Peace) is the nature of God. I see God as Shanthi. He has no form; He has no other name. He is all peaceful. He is all serenity. It is to be felt; it is to be experienced within one's self . . . When you are in Peace, you are in God. You are with God."

Meditation by Sri Swami Satchidananda,
Integral Yoga® Publications,
pages 11–12

Affirmation

You don't have to use Sanskrit words; you can use any word, or words, that are inspiring and uplifting to you—love and peace, health and happiness, courage and strength, peace and calm. Repeat one word with the inhalation and the other with the exhalation. You can just use one word if you prefer.

If you follow a particular religion or spiritual path, use a word, or words, that are meaningful to you from your tradition— Amen, Ameen, Shalom, Buddha Bhagavan, Allah, Wakan-Tanka.

Repeating Your Mantra

There are three ways to repeat a mantra or affirmation. If you are new to meditation, or if the mind is particularly distracted, repeat your mantra audibly. Repeat "hari om," for example, out loud, slowly and in a monotone voice.

When the mind becomes calm, repeat your mantra silently but with lip movement. This still gives the mind something more concrete to focus on and can help prevent it from wandering.

Eventually, repeat the mantra silently. With practice, you may hear the mantra without repeating it. In which case, just listen to the inner sound.

Meditation on the Breath

My partner Nick calls this the Martini Technique because you can use it anytime, any place, anywhere! Bringing the awareness to the breath helps to bring the mind into the present moment. It is great to use during the day whenever you feel stressed or upset or you just need to step back from your busy day.

1

Sitting comfortably, feel the floor beneath you. Make sure there is no unnecessary tension in the legs. Relax the belly. Lengthen through the spine, lifting the chest, and relaxing the shoulders down. Relax the face.

2

Take a deep breath in and out and then return the breath to normal.

3

Notice the movement of the body as you breathe.

4

Notice the sound of the breath.

5

Notice the length of the exhalation to the inhalation.

6

Finally, bring the awareness to the flow of breath at the tip of the nose and notice the cool air coming in and the warm air going out.

Ajapa-japa
(Meditation on the Sound of the Breath)

It is said that the breath makes a natural sound, repeating the mantra "soham" (the "a" is pronounced "u" as in "up").

1

Prepare as before and bring your awareness to the breath.

2

Mentally repeat "so" with the inhalation and "ham" with the exhalation.

3

With practice, if you listen carefully, you will hear "so" with the inhalation and "ham" with the exhalation without repeating the mantra.

4

In time you may hear a humming sound or musical note within. Concentrate on this sound. You are tuned into the hum or sound of the universe; vibrating at the same level as the cosmic vibration brings a deep sense of stillness, peace, and bliss.

Likhit Japa
(Writing Meditation)

This is another very useful technique if the mind is restless and sitting still is proving to be difficult. You can write your mantra or affirmation. You can write in a pattern or try to create a picture with your word or words. Keep the mind focused on the letters and the movement of the hand while mentally repeating each word. After you have finished writing, sit for a moment to notice how calm you feel.

Walking Meditation

If your mind is very restless and you find it difficult to sit still, go for a walking meditation. When walking and coordinating the breath with the movement, the mind and body become balanced, as do the right and left hemispheres of the brain. We are moving and thinking in harmony. After a walking meditation, you will find it much easier to sit still and meditate. You can practice a walking meditation at any time; you don't have to go out specifically to practice. Practice when walking to the store to get some milk, or when you go to mail a letter or walk from your car to your place of work.

1
Walk slowly and evenly.

2
Begin to incorporate the breath with your steps.

3
Breathe in as you step onto the right foot. Breathe out as you step onto the left foot.

4
If you want to you can begin to incorporate a mantra or affirmation, keeping the repetition in rhythm with your breath and step.

Self-Inquiry Meditation

- This is the process of asking yourself, "Who am I?"

- Go through the whole body asking, "Am I the arms?" "No." "I have arms, but that is not who I am." "Who am I?"

- After going through the body, go through all the labels you give yourself. For example, "Who am I?" "I am a teacher" "Were you a teacher when you were a child? Will you be a teacher when you retire?" "No." Go through everything that you think you are. "I am the Mind." "No." "You can observe the mind, so you are something other than the mind." "I am the thoughts." "No." You can watch the thoughts come and go. You can change your thoughts. You are something other than the thoughts.

- This is known as the neti-neti approach, "not this, not this." By negating everything that you think you are, you can see that these things are not permanent; they are ever-changing and therefore not real. In the process of negating everything that is not real, you ultimately end up with what is real, true, and permanent. You come to the realization that you are beyond the body and mind. The real you is absolute bliss and peace—that which is left when you strip away everything with which you falsely identify.

8

Yogic Diet

Yogic Diet

Everything we do in yoga is designed to bring physical ease and mental peace, and the yogic diet is no exception. A yogic diet will make the body light and easeful, the mind and emotions calm and steady, and improve clarity of thought and concentration. A yogic diet is known as a sattvic diet. It is easily digested, does not produce toxins, and consists mainly of fresh foods full of prana, our vital life force.

According to yogic philosophy, energy has three qualities called gunas—sattva (purity), rajas (activity), and tamas (inertia). In the unmanifest universe, these three qualities are in perfect balance. In the manifest universe, everything is made up from and affected by the three gunas, including our body, thoughts, emotions, and actions, but one of the three will always predominate. The only way to escape from the effects of the three gunas is to control the mind and transcend the lower self. The food we eat will be sattvic, rajasic, or tamasic and will affect our body, mind, and emotions. We are what we eat.

What to Eat

A sattvic diet includes fresh fruit and vegetables, whole grain cereals and breads, pulses and legumes, sprouted seeds, honey, milk, nuts, and seeds. The food should be neither too hot nor too cold, over- or undercooked, over- or underripe. If it is, its quality will change to rajasic or tamasic, and it will affect the body and mind in a negative way.

A rajasic diet stimulates the passions and causes restlessness and excitement in the mind; it makes the body stiff and ache with toxins, which can lead to disease. This type of diet will not help you to achieve a state of harmony. A rajasic diet consists of foods that are hot, spicy, salty, sour, bitter, and underripe. A rajasic diet also includes coffee, tea, chocolate, sugar, fish, eggs, and garlic.

A tamasic diet causes dullness and inertia in the body and mind, leading to a lack of creativity and motivation. It has a negative effect on the emotions and lowers the body's immunity. A tamasic diet consists of foods that are tinned, stale, overripe, overcooked, fermented, over-processed, and refined. It includes foods such as meat, onions, moldy cheeses, alcohol, tobacco, and fast foods.

The yogic diet recommends vegetarianism. This is because the human body is not really intended to eat meat. Our digestive system is not designed the same way as other meat-eating animals; our intestines are much longer, so it is not possible for the meat to pass through the digestive tract before it has putrefied. Red meat tends to clog up the digestive tract, producing toxins that break down the cells and cause decay in the intestines.

Sattvic, vegetarian food can pass through the digestive system and be eliminated within 24 hours; it takes red meat three to seven days. Meat contains 12 times more pesticides than vegetables, little if any fiber, and cholesterol, which thickens the arteries and can eventually cause atherosclerosis, high blood pressure, strokes, and heart attacks.

Research has proven that a bad diet, dietary imbalance, and the overconsumption of fat can affect your health more than anything else. Groundbreaking research by Doctor Dean Ornish has proved that yoga postures, relaxation, breathing practices, meditation, and a vegetarian, sattvic diet can heal heart disease (see bibliography).

In addition to the physiological reasons for being vegetarian, the yogi wants to practice harmlessness—ahimsa (see chapter 9). This means avoiding violence, and the pain and suffering caused to animals that are kept and killed for food. Could you bring a lamb home, kill it, and then eat it? Some people argue that we kill living organisms when we eat fruit and vegetables. However, a plant doesn't know it's being killed. The consciousness of a plant is lower than that of a cow. An animal knows when it is going to be killed. Its body reacts to the threat. It panics and introduces lots of adrenaline into its system—you are literally eating the fear and anxiety.

You don't need to change your diet overnight. However, you can make sensible, healthy choices. If you are going to eat meat, try to avoid red meat and processed meats, such as burgers and

Make healthy organic food choices.

sausages. Eat organic, free-range meat, chicken, fish, and eggs—at least the animals have had a happier life while being fattened up for your table. If you eat animal products, feel gratitude for the animal that has surrendered its life. The yogi would say a little prayer that its soul has attained eternal freedom and lasting peace because of its sacrifice.

How to Eat

How you eat is as important as what you eat. It can change the quality of sattvic food. For healthy digestion it is advisable to eat in a calm environment. If possible, eat your meal, or part of your meal, in silence. If you are upset or angry, it is better to wait until the emotions have calmed down because digestion will not be effective and food will linger in the stomach.

If you are angry while preparing the food, the vibration, or energy, of your thoughts will affect the vibration of your food, which in turn will have an effect when it is eaten. A yogi will chant peace mantras while preparing food and make sure that the environment is calm and peaceful. You don't have to go this far, but try to remain calm and enjoy preparing the food that will nurture you and your family, keeping you healthy and strong.

Chew your food well. Use all your teeth. Digestion begins in the mouth, where saliva begins to break down the food, putting less strain on the stomach. Don't stuff your mouth full and swallow big chunks of food.

Eat slowly. Rather than throw down a sandwich so you can get to an appointment on time, eat later. You will digest the food better and assimilate more goodness. When you eat slowly you will find that you can listen to the body telling you when it's had enough. People who eat fast tend to eat more and feel less satisfied. Eating in a hurry is rajasic.

Eat in moderation. Overeating is tamasic and will leave you feeling bloated and tired. Overeating can also lead to disease.

If you have a sensitive digestive system, you may find that it helps not to have cooked and raw foods at the same time. Some people find that mixing protein and

A sattvic diet helps maintain peace of mind.

carbohydrates in the same meal can also be taxing for the digestion.

Try not to drink with your meal, as this will dilute the digestive juices. Drink either before or after eating. However, make sure that you drink lots of water throughout the day. Water helps to cleanse the body of toxins, prevents constipation, and reduces the risk of contracting colon, bladder, and breast cancer. Did you know that even mild dehydration slows down the metabolism by up to 30 percent? Lack of water can be the cause of sleepiness during the day. Drinking 8–10 glasses of water a day, in a

lot of cases, can help to reduce back and joint pain. Fruit juice, tea, coffee, or soda drinks do not have the same effect as water. Some of them can actually cause dehydration, as well as adding toxins to your diet. Look at what happens to a plant when it is starved of water. The planet is 70 percent water and so are humans.

Eat before 8 PM if possible. The body has cycles and needs time for digestion, assimilation, and elimination. If you are always eating or you eat late at night, the body does not get to process and eliminate food effectively. You use more energy in digestion than for any other bodily function. If you go to bed on a full stomach, you will toss and turn to assist the process of digestion. Lack of rest means the body does not have the chance to properly rejuvenate itself.

Keep the mind focused on what you are doing. Concentrate on the flavors, textures, and smell. Think about where the food has come from. Feel a sense of gratitude for the food and be aware that it is nourishing the body and mind, giving you all that is needed for perfect health and happiness. Remember, as you think, so you become!

Fasting

Fasting is an important method for healing because it helps to rest the digestive system. In ideal conditions—when you are eating a sattvic diet—digestion takes about 15–30 percent of the body's energy. Under abnormal conditions, and particularly if you have a tamasic diet, it will use 90–95 percent. Whereas you will often feel tired after a "heavy" meal, a sattvic diet will leave you feeling refreshed. Our energy and concentration levels are at their highest when we are not eating.

Fasting helps to purify the body, it gives us control over the senses and calms the mind. When the body isn't receiving food, it will burn up, recycle, and eliminate toxins and fat, using up inner reserves. This is not starving the body and it is not a weight-loss diet. It is a method for preventing disease. Fasting can help eliminate the symptoms of diseases that start through the build up of toxins, such as rheumatism, arthritis, gout, diabetes, liver and kidney disease, asthma, and migraine. Fasting is also good for people with thyroid problems. The rest can help the metabolism to sort itself out. It should be noted that fasting is a complementary therapy for healing and not an alternative to traditional treatment.

Anybody over the age of 14 can fast. Children should not fast because they are

Fasting helps to purify the body, leading to strength and vitality.

growing and their metabolism is much faster. However, when children and adults are sick, it is a good idea to fast. You will heal much quicker with lots of water, nurturing, and love. Don't make people eat when sick; it is far better to let the body use its energy to heal itself rather than use it for digesting food.

Fasting will make the body feel light and comfortable. The mind will become alert and concentration will improve. The breath and perspiration will become sweet.

Types of Fast

Water is the most effective and the simplest way to cleanse the body of toxins, but may be a little too drastic if you are not used to it.

Fruit juice gives the body something a little more substantial. Make sure you use fresh fruit juice, preferably organic. You don't want to introduce anything artificial into the system when you are trying to clean it out. Make sure you don't gulp down a pint of juice all at once. Chew the juice and begin to break it down in the mouth before swallowing.

Buy a juicer to make your own organic veggie juices.

A fruit diet is a good way to fast if you have to keep working. Try to stick to one fruit at a time to make it easier for the body to digest and to get maximum benefit from the cleansing properties of the fruit. Melon and grapes are particularly cleansing and pineapple has wonderful enzymes, which are great for cleansing the digestive system.

If fasting for a whole day is too much, you can start with a half-day fast. Have a light meal in the evening and nothing else before going to bed, except maybe some water. Just drink herb tea or water all morning and then have a light lunch—fruit and yogurt, or lightly steamed vegetables or a light vegetable broth. This will give the system a good rest and allow the body an opportunity to throw out some accumulated toxins.

Fruit and vegetable juice fasts are a great way to help detox the body.

Preparing to Fast

- It is a good idea to fast one day a week. If possible, choose the same day and stick to it, preferably a day when you can rest and nurture yourself. Watch your favorite movie. Read a book you've been wanting to read for ages. Go on a gentle walk. Listen to relaxing music.

- Have a bath, but don't clog the pores with oils and cream. It is better to brush the skin with a rough towel or a soft brush to get rid of dead skin cells, clean the pores, and encourage the release of toxins.

- Don't use deodorant—again, we don't want to clog the pores—sweat away those toxins! Maybe just keep your distance from close friends for the day!

- Prepare yourself mentally and physically for the fast. Mark the date on your calendar and give yourself time to get used to the idea.

- Be careful not to binge the day before. This puts a tremendous strain on the system and will interfere with the positive effects of the fast. You won't be fasting; you'll simply be getting over the excesses of the day before. Make your last meal something light.

- If you have to help take care of your family, try and prepare their meals the day before so you don't have to spend too much time around food. There is no point fasting physically, if mentally you are eating all day long!

- Drink lots of water. This will help with elimination of toxins and can prevent you from feeling light-headed. A tablespoon of honey can help to stop you feeling spaced out.

While fasting, take time to nurture and pamper yourself.

- Some gentle yoga postures, deep relaxation, and breathing practices will help increase your energy and assist with the elimination process.

- Wear natural fibers, as these will absorb sweat and toxins. If you wear artificial fabrics they won't allow the skin to breath, and toxins can be reabsorbed back into the skin. Throw away that leopard-skin, lycra leotard and wear some loose cotton clothes instead.

Side Effects

- You may experience flatulence and a noisy tummy.
- Urine and perspiration may smell strange due to the elimination of toxins.
- Tongue and teeth may feel coated and the breath may smell at first. It's a good sign! In the mornings, gently scrape the tongue with the back of a teaspoon, or use a tongue scraper (available from all good yoga retail outlets). You'll be surprised at what you see. A lot of toxins are released through the tongue. It's a good idea not to eat or drink before you've cleaned the mouth; otherwise you are swallowing back the toxins.
- Some people experience headaches and/or nausea. Drinking water and deep breathing can help eliminate these feelings.
- You may feel tired or depressed— just rest. Do a deep relaxation or some deep breathing.
- You might get light-headed.
- You may feel cold. Keep body and feet cozy.

Breaking the Fast

This is perhaps more important than the fast itself. The fast will be a waste of time if, when you've finished, you stuff yourself with a burger and fries. If you're not careful, you can undo all the good you've done.

- Prepare yourself in advance. Plan and have ready at hand what you are going to eat and drink to break your fast before you start.

- If you fast for one day, take a whole day to get back to normal eating. If you fast for two days, take two days to break the fast and so on.

- Break the fast with something very light that will be easily digested. If you were on a water fast, take some fruit juice first. Drink it slowly, chewing the juice; don't just gulp it down. If you were fasting on fruit juice, then have some vegetable broth. Gradually increase your food intake and combinations.

- You might break a water fast with a herb tea for breakfast, fruit juice mid-morning, an apple for lunch, a banana mid-afternoon, and vegetable soup for supper.

- There's no point fasting if you are going to be miserable. Fasting for half a day until lunch will give the digestive system a good rest and ensure effective assimilation and elimination.

Finally

Don't worry about changing your diet overnight. The worry about what you are eating will probably cause you more harm than the food itself. Changes in what, how, and when you eat will happen gradually. Once you begin to enjoy the benefits of physical, mental, and emotional ease brought about through your yoga practice, you will find the desire for unhealthy things will diminish. Over time, your habits will change naturally without having to stress about it. Think of all the good you are doing and the benefits you are going to gain by developing a healthy, balanced diet. Gradually learn to eat the right things in the right quantity at the right time for you. Remember, with anything that you do in life, be happy, and have fun!

9

Yoga All Day and Every Day

Yoga All Day and Every Day

With regular yoga practice, you will soon begin to experience the benefits of health and a sense of inner calm and peace. These feelings will last after you have finished your session, but for how long?

What happens to your peace and calm when you see your cell phone bill? How long does your peace last when your siblings are fighting with you? Can you maintain your peace when your parents keep thinking they know best? Are you able to smile and be loving when your parents ask you to do the dishes? Can you remain contented when your friend at work gets the promotion instead of you? Are you able to accept graciously when your teacher piles a load of homework on your desk on Friday afternoon?

There is a story about a yogi who had been practicing for many years and was considered to be very wise. The yogi had mastered all the yogic techniques and had learned to control his emotions and mind, but felt that he hadn't dealt with anger in a sufficient way. "Shut me in this cave," he instructed the villagers, "and don't let me out or anybody in until I tell you." The wise

Can you keep calm under pressure?

yogi had decided to lock himself away from the world until he was able to control his anger. Days, weeks, and months went by, until one day the instruction was given to unblock the entrance to the cave. All the villagers gathered around to behold the enlightened Master. "Have you mastered your anger?" the villagers asked. Proudly the Master replied that he had. "Are you sure?" inquired a little boy. "Yes." "Are you really, really sure, you don't get angry any more?" "Yes." "What, really sure?" "YES," the so-called Master yelled!

Learn to adapt to any situation.

You need to be able to deal with the world and the people in it to be truly happy and to develop spiritually. In this final chapter, we will look at some simple tools to help you deal with the ups and downs of everyday life. Yoga provides you with a toolbox full of techniques and philosophical and psychological principles to help you keep the mind and emotions under your control, no matter what life throws at you. Familiarize yourself with all the tools, so you can use the right tool for the job at any given time. There is no point trying to undo a screw with a hammer; use the right tool and it's easy!

Yama and Niyama

In chapter 3, we looked at Raja yoga. Yamas and niyama are the first two limbs of this eight-limbed path to achieving the super-conscious state of samadhi. We shall now look at these moral and ethical principles in more detail.

Yama (Restraints)

Ahimsa (Harmlessness)

This is not just about not killing; we are talking about not harming anything or anyone by your thoughts, words, or deeds. You might say, "That's easy, I don't go around harming people and I'm kind to animals." Are you gentle with plants? Do you slam doors and bang drawers? Learn to walk and move gently, treating everything in a loving, gentle way. Generate a harmless vibration on the physical level first.

Now, what about your words? Sometimes a cruel or harsh word can cause just as much pain on an emotional level, as if you were to hit someone. In the *Bhagavad Gita*, another classical spiritual text on yoga, it says that speech should be non-harmful, truthful, beneficial, and pleasant. Create a harmless vibration with your speech.

Your actions and words may be harmless, but what about your thoughts? Your thoughts, like your words and actions, are energy, but in a more subtle form. Your thoughts affect every cell in your body and help create your mood. If you harbor

Cultivate divine, positive thoughts.

negative, harmful thoughts about someone, you don't hurt them but you end up hurting yourself, physically, emotionally, and mentally. You create negative energy, which attracts more negative energy, and you wonder why you feel depressed. To move on, leaving hurtful experiences behind, we have to learn to forgive, but harder still, we have to learn to forget. To relive painful experiences mentally is to relive them physically and emotionally.

You can substitute ahimsa for love. Learn to love everything and everybody unconditionally. Don't look for what is in it for you and don't concern yourself with what someone has or hasn't done to you. Don't give on the basis of what someone has given you; that's not love, that's more like a business arrangement. "I'll love you if you do this or give me that." This type of relationship will always bring misery, lack of satisfaction, and no contentment. Learn to love and give unconditionally, selflessly with no expectations. If you have some form of selfish expectation of someone, you are always going to end up disappointed. No one can make you happy all the time; you cannot rely on anyone or anything for your happiness, it's up to you.

Satya (Truthfulness)

Again this is in thought, word, and deed. If you always speak the truth, there comes a time when what you say comes true. Thoughts, words, actions, and material objects are all energy. Pure truthfulness or honesty is an aspect of the divine vibration. To practice and observe this quality is to manifest and attract this quality. Once established in satya, there is no more fear. There is nothing and no one to be afraid of; there is nothing to hide or avoid; you are completely open and at peace. The mind becomes clear and calm and reflects your true pure self.

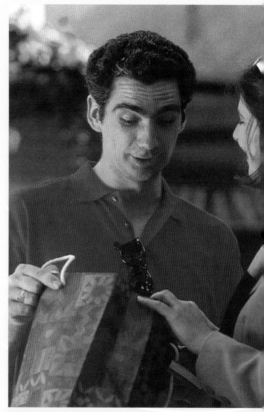

Being truthful.

To practice satya means to not tell white lies. If the truth will cause pain or trouble, keep quiet. If your mother is showing off her new dress, which you think is dreadful, what do you say? To tell her, "Mom, I wouldn't be seen dead in that" may be true, but it is harmful. To say, "Mom, that's wonderful, you're going to look like a million dollars" is a lie. What do you do? Think before you open your mouth; a wise man speaks little! Remember that as well as being truthful, your speech should be non-harmful, beneficial, and pleasant. Maybe you like the color of the dress or the style, so you can comment on that. Maybe you could say, "It's not as nice as that little black dress you wore last week." What is harmful to one person would be water off a duck's back to someone else. If you practice truthfulness and harmlessness, you will find that you speak the truth with love and compassion. Sometimes a little sugar helps the medicine to go down.

Asteya (Non-stealing)

We all know that it's wrong to steal and this moral restraint is found in all religious and spiritual paths. However, we are not just talking about stealing from a store or from someone's home. In some way or another we are all thieves. Think about it. We steal from nature every day. Every day we are given things. What do you give in return? A hug is a gift, so is a smile from a baby or a kind word. You don't have to give a hug back to the person who hugged you, but you could tidy your mother's bathroom or help an old man across the road. There are many ways to give back to nature.

We steal time from our boss. She pays us to work, and we spend half an hour on the telephone with a friend. We are stealing the boss's time and money. Have you ever taken pens from work? Have you ever used your friend's perfume without asking? We steal the use of things all the time, when we have more than we need. Rich countries steal from poor countries. How much food do we get rid of to keep prices competitive when there are people starving in other parts of the world? Do you have an old computer in your attic? You could say that you are stealing the use of that

computer from someone who needs one and can't afford a new one. Look at your life. Are you really practicing asteya?

Do we ask nature if we can eat her plants and animals or breathe her air? This doesn't mean that we should starve and stop breathing in the name of spiritual development! However, we should have respect for Mother Nature and utilize all that we are given to serve others. Nature gives selflessly everything that it has; we are part of nature, to live harmoniously we should learn to develop this selfless attitude. Does a cow produce milk and then drink it all? Does an apple tree produce sweet juicy fruit to enjoy them all itself? Do not take all the fruits of your work for yourself, but learn to give something in return. The yogi thanks Mother Nature every time she has something to eat or is given anything, saying something like, "Thank you for the food you have given me. May it make me healthy and strong so that I am a good person" or "Thank you for the pay raise.

May I use the money wisely for the benefit of my family."

Our greed makes us thieves. When we are given money, possessions, or love we want to lock them up or hang onto them, afraid of losing what we have gained. Never content with what we have, we always want more. Nature, however, is continually changing—things come and go. What happens if you try to stop the flow of a river? The pressure builds and builds until eventually it breaks free. If there is nothing obstructing the river, it flows in a torrent. If you develop a selfless attitude and allow things to come and go as they please, they tend to stay and more things tend to come. Don't disturb your mental peace through anxiety and fear of losing what nature has given you; you are only borrowing things temporarily. Sooner or later you will leave this body and all your possessions and money behind. Learn to be happy and content with what you have this moment. Don't worry about the past or future or you will miss the golden present. I heard someone say, "We call it the present because it's a gift." Enjoy the gift of life now—don't miss it.

Aparigrapha (Non-greed)

This follows on nicely from non-stealing because greed and hoarding, as we have seen, are a type of stealing. Some interpret aparigraha as "don't accept gifts." All the yama and niyama are designed so that we can live contented, happy, and peaceful lives. When we accept gifts from people, we often find ourselves in their debt or obliged to give or do something in return, even if that which is asked of us is not in keeping with what we would normally do or give. Sometimes the motive behind the act of giving is solely to get something in return; this is not a pure act and will lead to unrest.

Brahmacharya (Moderation)

Brahmacharya means to "put your attention on Brahman, the Absolute One." As we saw in the chapter on meditation, to attain the super-conscious state you first have to control the senses and then the mind. Yoga is about finding the "middle path" of moderation. Applying moderation is about learning to control the senses. The *Bhagavad Gita* says:

Moderation—in everything!

"It is impossible to practice yoga effectively if you eat or sleep either too much or too little. But if you are moderate in eating, playing, sleeping, staying awake, and avoiding extremes in everything you do, you will see that these yoga practices eliminate all your pain and suffering."

The Living Gita, Integral Yoga® Publications, 1988, pp. 89–90

Brahmacharya is also about celibacy. This is always controversial in our permissive society. Remember, yoga provides us with a toolbox for our free use. What tools do you need to use to maintain your peace? Use the tools that work for you and leave the rest in the box! If you were following a strict spiritual path, you would be asked to observe celibacy. The reason for this is to preserve energy, utilizing it for higher spiritual purposes. When you preserve energy, it gives physical and mental strength and vigor. It may be that celibacy is not going to be appropriate for you, but I would suggest that you look at moderation. Too much of anything depletes our stores of energy (see chapter 6). This can lead to weakness in the nervous system; a healthy nervous system is essential for our overall health and well-being.

Many people today are in the habit of consuming vast quantities of alcohol, drugs, chocolate, and food—as much of these things as they can get. Why?

There has always been permissive, "risky" behavior throughout the animal kingdom.

As basic survival is made easier, our animal instincts look for other ways of proving our strength and virility.

"Risky" behavior proves our strength and therefore our ability to survive and ensure the continuation of the species. The leader of a pack of animals may be challenged for leadership. The male that wins its fights will secure a female for mating.

Is the consumption of vast quantities of alcohol and drugs just another way of showing how strong we are in order to secure a mate?

Does excessive behavior really make you happy? Do you wake up on Monday morning and jump out of bed full of vitality and energy, ready to face the challenges of the week? There are always consequences to your actions. Maybe in your 20s and even your 30s, your body, mind, and emotions can cope with this abuse, but

there will come a time when excessive behavior will catch up with you. Save yourself a lot of pain and suffering later on in life by applying a little moderation now and reap the benefits of an easeful body, a peaceful mind, and a contented, useful life.

If you are indulging in excessive behavior, ask yourself why? Are you "numbing" yourself to avoid circumstances and situations that are causing pain and that you feel you cannot change? If this is the case and if you want to instigate change in your life, start today. First accept whatever is going on with your life. Painful, difficult situations are a blessing that serve to teach us great lessons; they make us more compassionate and more able to help others. Face the challenges of life; don't run away from them, as they will follow you wherever you hide. Begin to implement some of the teachings in this book. Little by little, learn to cleanse the body and calm the mind—and I promise, a new, brighter day will dawn for you. Like clouds that hide the sun temporarily—everything passes.

Niyama (Observances)

Saucha (Purity)

For serious spiritual seekers there comes a point when the attention is drawn away from the physical body and turned toward God. Less time is spent on grooming and preening and the desire for physical gratification and union with another is diminished.

This might not be applicable to us right here and now, but there is a level at which practicing saucha can enhance the quality of our life. Purifying the body through Hatha postures, breathing practices, and a yogic diet will eliminate tension and aches and pains and help to prevent serious disease. Purifying the mind with these techniques and the practice of meditation helps us to have a more positive, brighter outlook on life. When we become pure, nothing is disgusting to us. Real purification is to see everything in its purity. If we focus on purity, then purity comes to us. Learn to see the good in others. You see what is wrong, bad, or impure because you have the eye to see it; that is how your mind works. A holy person will only see what is good and pure and will accept and love all

A room free of clutter helps us develop purity.

unconditionally. As well as practicing yoga to develop purity of body and mind, make your surroundings clean, neat, and tidy. Get rid of clutter—a cluttered room or closet reflects the clutter in your mind.

Samtosha (Contentment)

Contentment is one of the greatest gifts or blessings that can be bestowed upon us. If you are contented, there are no likes or dislikes. There is nothing to get or gain and there is nothing to lose. With contentment we experience supreme joy; we no longer have to look outside ourselves for happiness. Contentment is greater than happiness as there is no opposite waiting around the corner. Contentment makes our life simple. Contentment is accepting what is. Everything in life eventually passes, so what we call good or bad will pass and bring either pleasure or pain. Contentment is beyond the duality of everyday life. Stop trying to change people, accept them as they are; this can transform relationships. Start with accepting and loving yourself and then your family. Possessions, relationships, youth—everything changes sooner or later. However, if you have contentment, you will always have peace.

Contentment is a blessing.

Tapas (Austerity)

Tapas means to burn or to purify. Through fasting, we burn away toxins and excess fat from the physical body; through meditation and learning to control the mind, we practice mental tapas; through practicing silence, verbal tapas, we learn to control the speech. To purify, we need to generate heat to burn away impurities. For example, the longer gold ore is burned, the purer it becomes, until we get 24-carat gold. It takes a truck full of ore to get 1 oz. (28 grams) of pure gold. When we burn away our impurities, we get to our pure essence.

Tapas means accepting but not causing pain. If someone causes us pain, the suffering will help to purify our bodies and minds. No one can upset you and disturb your peace if you accept the suffering in this way. We always gain something through accepting but not returning pain. It's a great test to see how mentally strong and peaceful you have become. Taking out your pain on someone else does not produce spiritual growth.

Do not cause pain to yourself, harming the temple of the divine. There is enough pain in life without creating more yourself. When we accept and see the reason for pain it goes. Embrace pain and let it go as quickly as possible—not as pain but as something to grow from.

Accept, then let go of pain.

Svadhyaya (Spiritual Study)

Read something every day that will inspire you and help to transform your life and attitudes. Read about the lives of great people. Study the beauty and miracle of nature. Any spiritual practice performed regularly is spiritual study. Begin to make everything your study. Observe and learn.

Try and read something spiritually significant every day.

Isvara Pranidhanam (Surrender)

To totally surrender is as difficult as loving everything with thought, word, and deed. Practice one or the other and everything in life falls into place. Become childlike and surrender to someone, or something, higher and purer than yourself. Begin with surrendering to someone who knows more. Be humble and learn what he or she has to teach. Eventually you will be able to surrender to your higher self; humbling the ego, quietening the mind, being able to listen to your higher will, or conscience. The ego may help to get you many things, but it won't get you peace.

Vairagya (Non-attachment)

Many people misunderstand non-attachment and think it means that you are indifferent and don't care. This is not correct. Vairagya is to have a calm mind free from personal, selfish desire. In *The Yoga Sutras*, Patanjali tells us that there are two main types of thoughts—those that are painful and those that are painless. My Guru would say that you could change this to, "thoughts that are selfish or selfless." If you have a selfish desire or expectation, you will always end up in pain or upset.

Look at your own life and see the truth in this. When you are upset, examine the cause and you will find that you had some selfish expectation or desire. You may have to look hard, but when you've finished blaming other people and other things, look at yourself and you will find selfishness. Gurudev would say, "When you are pointing the finger at someone else, look at how many are pointing back at you!" Selfishness and uncontrolled desires bring us misery. Practice contentment and non-greed and learn to reduce your wants.

Often the cause of your unhappiness comes from within.

The Four Locks and Four Keys

The following advice comes from Book One, Sutra 33. This sutra is of immense value when it comes to maintaining peace and happiness in life. Basically, there are four main types of people that we come across (4 locks) and four attitudes we can develop to remain calm and peaceful (4 keys).

FOUR LOCKS	FOUR KEYS
Happy	Friendliness
Unhappy	Compassion
Virtuous	Delight
Wicked	Disregard

If someone is happy because they've got a new house or a better job, be happy and friendly toward them. Jealousy, hatred, and looking for something negative about the happy person are very common ways to behave. What you might notice is that whenever you are jealous because of someone else's good fortune you only end up disturbing yourself.

When someone is unhappy, try to be compassionate. Listen to them. So often we do not have the time for someone who is sad. We justify our selfish behavior by saying that, "They brought it on themselves" or "I told them so!" This attitude will not help to cultivate peaceful thoughts and vibrations in the mind. Sometimes just giving an unhappy person a hug or touching their arm can give a strong message that someone cares and is there for them.

Listen to people.

When you come across virtuous people, delight in their good qualities and try to develop them in your life. So often we envy or criticize such people, trying to knock them off the pedestal that we put them on in the first place.

Sometimes, no matter how you try to help someone, or point out a better way to behave, it just doesn't make any difference. If there are people in your life who continually disturb your peace of mind, walk away. Don't waste your time and energy trying to "sort them out." If people want help, they will ask; if they are not ready to listen or learn, there is nothing you can do. Learn from these people; they are showing you how not to behave if you want to have a happy and healthy life. Have compassion. Angry, violent, or unlawful people are not usually happy people. Don't shout and "get your own back," but just calmly walk away. Don't waste energy going over and over situations in your mind, you are only upsetting yourself. As you walk away physically, you must learn to walk away mentally as well.

Don't let others' behavior cloud your own.

Pratipaksha Bhavana (Raising the Opposing Thought)

This is one of my favorite techniques for keeping a contented calm and peaceful mind. It can be found in Book Two, Sutras 33 and 34 of Patanjali's *Yoga Sutras*.

When a negative thought comes into the mind, raise the opposite, positive thought.

Change the scene!

One negative thought will lead to another, which will lead to another, and before you know it, you're in a downward spiral, spinning headfirst into depression. If you are feeling sad, think of the word happiness. You may not feel happy, but that doesn't matter. Remember, as you think, so you become. Fake it till you make it! By continually thinking your happy thought, you will eventually change your emotional mood and indeed the vibration of your entire body. If you are experiencing a lack of love, repeat the word love and again you will change your outlook.

As well as changing your thoughts, it is a good idea to change your environment. If you are angry or upset, go to a place where you feel calm or happy. If you can't leave the house and you have been angry in the kitchen, go to your bedroom or sit in your meditation room or corner; the energy will be different, and this will help you to calm down. Take a few deep, three-part breaths and repeat your positive word— watch your mood change. You can always go to a place where you were happy in your mind. Concentrate on the place and how you felt when you were there; take some deep breaths and repeat a positive word.

Spread the Love

Yoga is concerned with developing and changing the individual. If you don't have peace in your mind, how can you hope to have peace within your family? If you don't have peace within your family, how can you hope to have peace on the planet? Start with yourself. Take small steps and have fun. Apply these wonderful teachings to your life and experience peace in the midst of turmoil. Spread a little love and happiness and watch it grow. Laugh. Laugh at yourself. When you feel yourself getting uptight or anxious, laugh. Fake laughter has been proved to have the same beneficial effects as real laughter. Laughter is social medicine. It relieves stress, boosts the immune system, and releases endorphins that produce a natural high. Put a sticker above your place of work, "In case of emergency, laugh." Buy a joke book and every time you get anxious, read a joke. Remember those wise words of Monty Python, "Always look on the bright side of life!"

When you can walk around with a loving, smiling face, you will know that you are growing spiritually. Don't concern yourself about seeing bright lights, visions, or levitating off the floor in your meditations. Don't be concerned about sitting in the Full Lotus Pose. Just learn to love all, serve all, and smile. Rise above all the petty differences and prejudices of the lower nature and see the divine in all. Bring happiness and harmony wherever you go. Be of use. Make a difference, no matter how small, and you will experience heaven on earth.

Bibliography

The Yoga Sutras of Patanjali, translation and commentary by Sri Swami Satchidananda, Integral Yoga Publications, 1997.

The Living Gita, The Complete Bhagavad Gita, by Sri Swami Satchidananda, Integral Yoga Publications, 1988.

Sri Swami Satchidananda: Apostle of Peace, by Sita Bordow and others, Integral Yoga Publications, 1986.

Meditation, by Sri Swami Satchidananda, Integral Yoga Publications, 1975.

The Healthy Vegetarian, by Sri Swami Satchidananda, Integral Yoga Publications, 1986.

The Healing Path of Yoga, by Nischala Joy Devi, Three Rivers Press, 2000.

Stress, Diet and Your Heart, Dr. Dean Ornish, New American Library, 1982.

Beast and Man, by Mary Midgley, Routledge, 1979.

Autobiography of a Yogi, by Paramahansa Yogananda, Rider Books, 1946.

Index

Credits and Acknowledgements

Eternal love and gratitude to Gurudev, the real author of this book.

I would like to thank my teachers, Nischala Joy Devi and Swami Vidyananda, for their dedication and love. Thank you to Swami Sharadananda, my teacher, guide and friend, for your love and continual help. Thank you for always being there to answer my every question with patience, clarity, wisdom, and a sense of humor!

Thank you to my beloved fiancé Nicholas for reminding me when it is time to eat and for always being there with a cuddle just when I need it most!

Thank you to my wonderful students Nischala Pearson and Marco de Figueiredo, for being such fun and patient models for this book.

Thank to Sarah and David King for giving me the opportunity to share the glorious teachings of yoga with you.

Contacts

Integral Yoga®
Satchidananda Ashram
Yogaville
Route 1, Box 1720
Buckingham, VA 23921
http://www.yogaville.org

Integral Yoga® Institute of Montreal
5425 Avenue de Parc
Montreal, QC H2V 4G9
Canada
(514) 271-1633
winds@total.net

Picture Credits

Pages 10, 11, 16, 23, 30, 35, 39–40, 47–49, 54, 138, 140, 161–162, 166, 204, 208, 212, 221–225, 227–229, 242 © Getty Images; pp. 19, 24–29, 32–34, 36–37, 42, 142, 145, 147, 149, 162–163, 184, 191, 201, 215, 220, 230, 232–238, 240, 243–249 © Stockbyte.